THE
DIAMOND
DAKOTA
MYSTERY

THE DIAMOND DAKOTA MYSTERY

Juliet Wills
with Marianne van Velzen

ALLEN&UNWIN

*This work contains images of deceased Aboriginal people.
We regret any sadness this may cause relatives and
community members.*

First published in 2006

Allen & Unwin
83 Alexander Street
Crows Nest NSW 2065
Australia
Phone: (61 2) 8425 0100
Fax: (61 2) 9906 2218
Email: info@allenandunwin.com
Web: www.allenandunwin.com

*National Library of Australia
Cataloguing-in-Publication entry:*

Wills, Juliet.
The diamond Dakota mystery.

Bibliography.
Includes index.
ISBN 978 1 74114 745 2

ISBN 1 74114 745 X.

1. Palmer, Jack. 2. Larceny - Western Australia - Beagle
Bay. 3. World War, 1939–1945 - Western Australia - Broome -
Aerial operations, Japanese. I. Title.

364.162099414

Map by Ian Faulkner
Set in 12/18 pt Adobe Garamond by Bookhouse, Sydney
Printed in Australia by McPherson's Printing Group

10 9 8 7 6 5 4 3 2

For William, Becky and Sam

CONTENTS

PART TWO   Diamonds galore

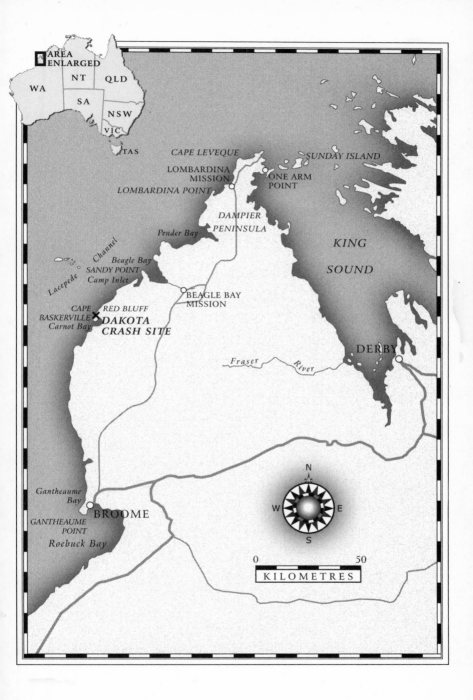

PREFACE

As an investigative journalist, occasionally you find a diamond of a story—one that glitters more brightly than the rest. Trawling through historical documents at the Battye Library in Western Australia, while working on another story, I discovered my diamond: the intriguing story of beachcomber 'Diamond' Jack Palmer, pilot Captain Ivan Smirnoff, and a missing cache of diamonds.

My children have been raised on Australian legends like Lasseter's lost reef of gold and the treasures of the *Gilt Dragon* shipwreck, and the tale of missing diamonds on a remote coastline struck me as a story of similar magnitude, the type that could become etched into Australian folklore for generations to retell. I couldn't believe that such an amazing tale, full of vibrant characters, intrigue and sorrow, was not already common knowledge.

Diamond Jack embodied characteristics that Australians have so often identified with: larrikinism and bold dreams. Like the bushrangers of colonial Australia, he shared a disdain for rules, rituals and regulations, but unlike Harold Lasseter's reef, there was no question of the existence of Palmer's fortune. And his playgrounds were not the teeming cities, sheep stations or desert, but a vast and remote coast that continues to inspire the imagination and challenge those who dare to venture along it. But this is much more than a tale of larrikins and lost treasure; it also serves to honour the memory of those who died in one of the most tragic events to unfold on Australia's shores—the air raid on Broome on 3 March 1942 and the subsequent attack on the Diamond Dakota above the Kimberley coastline.

As I began to search through archived documents, books and newspapers, I found myself following in the wake of a Dutch journalist, Marianne van Velzen, absorbed in the same world of pearlers, pilots, survival, death, tragedy and treasure on the rugged and beautiful north-west coast of Australia.

She had put many pieces of the puzzle together for a Dutch television documentary, accessing information available in The Hague and elsewhere in the Netherlands and Australia. We agreed that together, working from opposite ends of the world, we could give the most comprehensive and detailed view both of the tragedy that unfolded for Dutch refugees in Broome, Australia, in 1942, and of the story of the missing diamonds. Her research, assistance and advice have been invaluable.

I have striven for historical accuracy at all times, but in some instances survivors' accounts differ and I have had to choose between the two. Conversations and events in the text have been reconstructed based on police statements, trial notes, newspaper and historical accounts, books and personal recollections. While there is no record of conversations that took place in the Javasche Bank on the night the diamonds were moved from Bandung, I have reconstructed this scene based on intelligence documents held in Commonwealth Bank archives, documents tendered at the trial of Jack Palmer, James Mulgrue and Frank Robinson, and interviews with the children of Willy Olberg and David Davidson. Conversations between the survivors at Carnot Bay have been reconstructed based on Smirnoff's autobiography—*De Toekomst heeft Vleugels* (The Future has Wings)—Anne Coupar's biography of Smirnoff, Leon Vanderburg's account in William Tyler's *Flight of Diamonds*, a Dutch newspaper interview with Jo Muller and my interview with Pieter Cramerus, the only survivor of the Carnot Bay crash still known to be alive at the time of writing this book.

Conversations on the beach at Pender Bay are reconstructed based on trial notes, intelligence documents, army records and Mulgrue's written account of the event, held by the Broome Historical Society. Mulgrue's discussion of pearling at the bar in Broome was taken from the book *The Pearl Seekers*, where the author, Norman Bartlett, recounted a conversation with an old 'Indian Army Captain'. To my knowledge, Mulgrue was the only man who fitted this description in Broome in the

1940s. Further details regarding the sources of information are contained in the bibliography.

Please note that in referring to the people that made up Broome's colourful society, I have used the terminology of the day, hence Manilamen, Koepangers, Javanese and Malays, as nations such as Indonesia and the Philippines were yet to gain independence.

PROLOGUE

David Davidson and his brother-in-law Sloume (Willy) Olberg peered around nervously. The room was dark; the windows had been blacked out and a small lantern let off only spare light. The manager of the Javasche Bank sat behind a large wooden desk. The director of the Netherlands Exchange Institute of the Javasche Bank stood nearby.

'The situation is hopeless,' the director told them. 'The full-scale evacuation is in its final stages. The bank has already moved much of its gold reserves to Australia. As your company is one of the bank's most important clients we suggest that you, too, consider the transport of your holdings. We do not want the Japanese to be any better resourced than they already are.'

The news that the Japanese had landed on Java had sent a wave of shock across the island. More than 300 years of colonial Dutch rule was coming to an end—and Bandung, celebrated as the Paris of Java because of its spectacular parks, wide boulevards and beautiful Art Deco buildings—was now teeming with soldiers; the incessant sounds of gun fire and exploding bombs filled the air.

Davidson and Olberg's company, N.V. de Concurrent, had traded from the grandest shop on the Jalan Braga since 1914, offering the finest of European silverware, jewellery, watches, gold and precious stones. Forced from their homes in Amsterdam when the Nazis invaded the Netherlands, they had stocked up on supplies of diamonds and gold when they fled to the East Indies.

The director advised the two men that the Exchange Institute had negotiated with the Commonwealth Bank, which then acted as the Reserve Bank of Australia, for the secure transfer of East Indies wealth stored at the Javasche Bank to a secret storage facility in the Australian outback should Java fall. The director explained that the transport of their wealth to Australia was their best hope of retaining some control over their assets.

David Davidson shifted his broad frame in his chair, rubbing his stubby fingers across his balding forehead—the thought of the impending Japanese invasion filled him with fear. His wife was due to have a baby any day now and he had three other young children at home. He could not leave Bandung and just prayed the Japanese would be merciful.

Willy Olberg had known this was coming. His only son, Frans, whom he hoped would take over the family business, had joined up to fight the Japanese onslaught. He did not want to abandon him. His seventeen-year-old daughter, Elly, had been sent to stay with relatives in the mountains, away from the major settlements, where Willy hoped she would be safe.

'What do we need to do?' Olberg asked.

'We have the paperwork organised. Can you give us an estimate of the value of your holdings?'

'Diamond appraisal is a precise task which takes time,' Davidson explained.

'Speaking of time, we must get moving!' The bank's manager moved quickly to the door.

Davidson followed and the two men walked down the stairs to the steel door of the vault. The banker opened the door and Davidson went inside to retrieve his safety deposit box. Returning to the dark office, the men huddled around as Davidson opened the lid and removed thousands of diamonds. Willy Olberg cleaned his glasses and then set to work, swiftly separating the stones into sixty-five small parcels, each one containing approximately twenty carats' worth of diamonds. The larger ones, those of more than seven carats, had been destined for wealthy clients such as the Sultan of Deli.

There were too many diamonds and not enough time to count precisely how many went into each parcel. The parcels were wrapped in pale blue tissue paper and placed into compartments of a leather jewellery wallet. The bulging wallet was placed into a strawboard box, slightly larger than a cigar box. The bank manager lifted the precious box and wrapped it carefully in white paper, tying it with string. The words 'Commonwealth Bank, Sydney' were scrawled across the top.

Holding the sealing wax close to the flame of the lantern, the banker patiently waited for the wax to soften, then carefully rubbed it on the package in a circular motion until there was enough to apply the seal. The official logo of 'De Javasche Bank—Bandoen' was then impressed into the wax. He repeated the motion and Davidson pressed down a second seal bearing N.V. de Concurrent's emblem: a crown. The director then placed a document before Davidson and Olberg for them to sign. They glanced over the words, then signed the paperwork, eager to get moving. At this point, both men were more concerned for their own safety and the safety of their families than for their wealth.

'Good luck,' the director said. They all knew they would need plenty of that to survive the coming days.

Part One

FLIGHT, DEATH AND SURVIVAL

Chapter One

EVACUATION

2 MARCH 1942, JAVA, NETHERLANDS EAST INDIES

Oil dripped from the engine of the Douglas DC-3 Dakota and sizzled on the steamy tarmac. Dutch pilot Captain Ivan 'Turc' Smirnoff sought shade under the wing of the aircraft, but it offered little respite from the stifling heat and humidity. The atmosphere at Andir airport seemed surreal and terrifying to Smirnoff and his crew, who anxiously waited for their passenger load and further instructions. Occasional machine-gun fire could be heard from the other side of the mountain pass, adding to their unease. Wrecked hangars and the remains of planes smouldered around them, a constant reminder of the danger they were in.

Soldiers on the outskirts of the airport terminal allowed through only those whose names were on the evacuation list. The plane's passenger load was limited, and military personnel who could continue the fight against the Japanese would be given priority. The civilian and military passengers selected for evacuation sat nervously in the terminal, aware of the many people outside desperate to take their place. Everyone wanted to get moving.

The aircraft radiated the sun's heat and Smirnoff's uniform was wet with perspiration. The morning passed and the midday sun beat down through thick tropical clouds and still there was no word from military officials. The wait was excruciating. Time seemed to be moving in slow motion, out of sync with the action unfolding around them.

Smirnoff wished the clouds would break to ease the oppressive heat. A strong wind whipped up, blowing hats, bending trees and lifting the plane from its chocks. The Dakota looked as if it was champing at the bit. Thunder and lightning cracked in the distance, drowning out the gun fire. In peacetime no pilot would take to a sky so laden with monsoonal clouds. But this was war.

As Imperial Russia's second most decorated pilot in the First World War, Ivan Smirnoff was considered to be daring, cool and uncannily lucky by fellow pilots. He had shot down eleven German planes, a phenomenal number for the Eastern Front, and his bravery had earned him a raft of honours and the nickname 'Ivan the Indestructible'. His medals included the Croix de Guerre, the Cross of St George (awarded when he was a foot soldier), the White Eagle of Siberia and the Order of St George for exceptional bravery (the equivalent to the Victoria Cross).

The flight of refugees from war-torn countries was an all-too-familiar scenario for Smirnoff, who had been forced to flee his homeland after the Russian Revolution in 1917. He eventually ended up in England, where he joined the Royal Air Force. At the end of the First World War he joined KLM Royal Dutch Airlines. These were the pioneering days of civil aviation, when the endurance of planes and pilots was put to the test and when many didn't make it. Pilots such as Charles Lindbergh, Charles Kingsford Smith and Amelia Earhart took to the skies, breaking new ground and becoming media celebrities. Smirnoff became a famous international pilot in his own right, breaking record after record in the air, and was soon a household name in his newly adopted home. In 1933 he had flown what was then the longest air route in the world in just four days; it was a trip which normally took ten. The story made newspaper headlines around the globe.

The war in Europe had forced Smirnoff and his wife, Danish actress Margot Linnet, from their home in Amsterdam and the pair had relocated to the Dutch East Indies. Java was to be a haven away from the horror of war in Europe. But after the Japanese invasion of Pearl Harbor on 7 December 1941, Smirnoff was mobilised to help the Allies defend the Pacific.

The world was surprised by the speed at which the Japanese had been able to move through the Pacific. Singapore was attacked at almost the same time as Pearl Harbor, and within two days Japanese attacks on RAF fields in Singapore had destroyed nearly all of the RAF's front line aeroplanes. Vital aerial support for the army was lost before the actual ground attack on Singapore had even begun. The British forces never had time to regroup, and predictions of an attack by sea proved fatally wrong.

Lacking aerial support, the flagships of the British Navy, *Prince of Wales* and the battle cruiser *Repulse*, the Allies' principal defence, were unable to fend off repeated attacks from Japanese torpedo bombers and were sunk. These were the first of the capital ships sunk solely by air power while actively resisting attack. British Prime Minister Winston Churchill later said of the event, 'In all of the war I have never received a more direct shock.'

By the end of December, the Japanese had captured the Philippines, Guam, Wake Island and Hong Kong; Malaya fell on 11 January 1942 and, on 8 February, 23,000 Japanese soldiers attacked Singapore across the Johore Strait. Nearly 150,000 young men were captured and one in four would not survive the three and a half long years to war's end.

With all of Malaya and southern Sumatra under their control, the Japanese now concentrated on the islands and sea expanses of the East Indies, the last barrier between them and Australia. All along, the oil-rich East Indies had been one of their primary targets. The Americans had placed an oil embargo on the Japanese to protest their aggression in China. But the Japanese needed oil to fulfil their imperialistic goals. The full might of the Japanese army, navy and air force was now bearing down on Java.

The Allies proved no match for the Japanese. In a dramatic battle on the Java Sea on 27 February 1942, almost the entire Allied fleet was sunk within a few hours, while the Japanese escaped virtually unscathed. More than 2000 men lost their lives.

With Java now almost certain to fall, chaos and confusion erupted as terrified people sought passage further south to Australia and elsewhere.

The roads leading to and from the port were blocked with floods of people trying to escape by sea. Pilots all over Java prepared to move out their aircraft and as many military and civilian personnel as possible, principally through Australia. Even though Darwin had been bombed on 14 February 1942, to the people trapped on Java just about anywhere else seemed safer. Dutch flying boats were hidden at isolated rivers and dams, waiting for the cover of night.

When Smirnoff arrived back from an evacuation run to Sydney the night before, he was unaware that the Japanese had already landed on Java. In the early hours of the morning, invading forces had launched a three-pronged assault on the island. Poorly resourced defenders had no chance of fending off the attack and the Japanese were now marching on Bandung and Batavia. As soon as Smirnoff had landed, military officials ordered him to hide his aircraft until the next day as they attempted to coordinate the mass evacuation of the island. His Douglas DC-3 Dakota, the *Pelikaan*, had been refuelled, flown to a concealed airstrip and camouflaged. At daybreak, after a few hours' nap, Smirnoff and his crew—co-pilot Johan 'Neef' Hoffman, radio operator Jo Muller and aircraft mechanic Joop Blaauw—had returned to Andir airport, flying under cover of cloud. They were still awaiting further instructions.

There was no news on exactly how close the invading forces were but they weren't far away. Every hour the Allied forces could keep the Japanese at bay increased the chance of escape for those few lucky enough to be squeezed on board a ship or plane before the inevitable occupation. It was just a matter of time.

By now, the twilight had been lost in the stormy, blackened sky which blurred the passing of day to night. One by one on the hour, aeroplanes had taken off into the thunderous sky, yet still Smirnoff stood on the tarmac under the metal wings of his aircraft. Agitated people continued to argue with harried officials for places on planes. Against orders, some pilots with empty seats dashed off to get their families. Smirnoff was glad that Margot was safe and settled in Australia.

The clouds burst and heavy drenching rain pelted down, helping to drown out the sound of gun fire which had become louder and closer. Having completed their pre-flight checks the crew sought shelter in the cabin. The Japanese invasion forces were moments away and they were beginning to feel that the *Pelikaan* might well be the last plane left on Java.

Finally, at around 11.30 p.m., the *Pelikaan*'s passengers made their way across the tarmac and mounted the stairs. Young and fresh-faced, Dutch Air Force Pilot Sergeant Leon Vanderburg was relieved to receive the phonecall ordering him to the airport for evacuation. He had been fighting on the front-line and watched all too many friends fall to the Japanese. The Allies had sent many pilots to defend Java, but there were few service-able aircraft for them to fly. He hurried to the airport and quickly spotted the DC-3. He shook Smirnoff's hand and boarded the plane.

For passenger Pieter Cramerus, it had been the most terrifying and eventful day of his life. When he and his commanding officer, Lieutenant Commander Johannes Beckman, had driven north from Bandung to Kalidjati Air Base early that morning they had no idea the Japanese had landed. The road had seemed uncannily quiet as they made their way north past the Tangkuban Parahu volcano and on through pineapple and tea plantations. The quiet came to an abrupt end when the pair were stopped by Japanese soldiers and captured. Cramerus had managed to escape, but Lieutenant Commander Beckman was decapitated five days after he was captured.

Reporting to headquarters at Bandung after his escape, Cramerus was told he would be put on the urgent evacuation list and to make his way to the airport.

Dutch naval pilots Dick Brinkman and Heinrick Gerrits also climbed on board, as did a young, fit KNILM (East Indies airlines) employee with white hair, Hendrick van Romondt.

Pilots, mechanics and wireless operators were given priority passage, but leftover seats were given to women and children. Smirnoff advised he could take one more passenger. Charlie van Tuyn, an engineer on a Lodestar, had told his wife Maria to be ready to go with their young son, Jo. When she was advised by the official in the airport that there was a spot for her, she was filled with relief. The official pointed to Smirnoff's plane and she hurried out the door, clutching her baby boy, towards the darkened outline of the *Pelikaan*.

As the gracious 25-year-old Dutchwoman approached the plane carrying her wide-eyed son, Smirnoff smiled. He'd spoken to Charlie van Tuyn earlier in the day; he was desperate to get his family out. She brushed aside her blonde hair and thanked Smirnoff for agreeing to take them to safety.

Dutch pilot Daan Hendriksz, already on board, was surprised at the arrival of Maria van Tuyn. He had noted women and children being smuggled onto the other planes, but it was too late to drive back to the plantation to collect his pregnant seventeen-year-old wife, Jacqueline. The night before, he had drifted in and out of sleep. He dreamt the plane he was in was under attack and burst into flames. That everyone around him was screaming. He cried out, waking Jacqueline. Unable to sleep, they had discussed their options. There didn't seem to be any. Staying was dangerous and so was leaving. Then the phonecall came ordering him to the airport for evacuation. Between the premonition, Jacqueline's pregnancy and a presumption that the pilot would be unwilling to take responsibility for civilian lives, Hendriksz had opted to leave Jacqueline with her family on the plantation near Bandung. But now, as he witnessed other women boarding the planes, he wished he had brought her with him.

Maria van Tuyn was offered the only seat on the DC-3; all the others had been removed to minimise weight. The co-pilot, Neef Hoffman, would join the other passengers and crew relegated to the uncomfortable wooden floor.

Out of the cockpit window, Maria could see only one plane left on the tarmac. It was Charlie's plane, a Lockheed Lodestar piloted by Gus Winckel. As it took off into the night sky, she wondered if he was as anxious about this flight as she was. It would be a great relief to see Charlie's face in Broome.

A ban on communication meant the airwaves were silent, but Jo Muller continued to listen for transmissions. Mechanic Joop Blaauw closed the cabin door as Captain Smirnoff, three crew members, and eight passengers prepared for take-off.

Lightning flashed around them and the night sky faded to black before the signal came to leave. Just as Smirnoff was about to start the engines, the door burst open and a gust of air swept through the cabin, blowing the cap off Hoffman's head. The group, already on edge, jumped at the intrusion. A red-faced man stood puffing in the doorway of the aircraft. Gathering his breath, he yelled out to catch the captain's attention, stepping over the passengers seated on the wooden floor. The last thing anyone on board wanted or needed was another delay. But the man ignored the agitated passengers and moved towards the cockpit. 'I know you're eager to get going, Captain, but this is urgent.' He handed Smirnoff a package wrapped in white paper with two impressive wax seals on it. 'It's very valuable,' he said. Normally, such a package would have documentation with it, but this was not a night for formalities or questions. Smirnoff threw it down beside him, to the obvious alarm of the red-faced man.

'Take very good care of it. It has great value,' he insisted, without disclosing its contents. 'An Australian bank will take delivery of it in Sydney.' Smirnoff placed it in the little cabinet containing his briefcase and confidential documents, and the man nodded with approval. 'Guard it safely!' the man repeated, then wished the pilot well, clambered back over the passengers and left the plane. The door was again sealed. Smirnoff hoped there would be no more delays.

Simultaneously engaging the starter and primer switches, Smirnoff waited for the propellers to turn four revolutions before the Wright Cyclone engines awoke one cylinder at a time, belching and coughing smoke. The plane groaned and creaked as it taxied into position ready for take-off. To Smirnoff, who had spent so long waiting to get going, the groans of the Douglas sounded like a song. He completed the last minute pre-flight checks before moving down the runway over bomb craters that had been hastily filled in earlier. As he released the brakes and advanced the throttle, the *Pelikaan* climbed into the night sky. It was now 1.15 a.m. local time. Only one other plane would make it out from Andir airport that night.

The thunderclaps and lightning melded with the roaring of the guns as the defenders on the outer perimeter of Bandung attempted to keep the Japanese at bay, a frightening sound-and-light show as the weather played to the drama on the stage below. Black clouds and driving rain soon cut all visibility. Smirnoff would have to navigate the high mountains around Bandung using only his instruments.

As the plane banked to the south, heading for Broome on the north coast of Australia, Captain Smirnoff breathed a sigh of relief; they were finally on their way.

Chapter Two

DESTRUCTION

3 MARCH 1942, BROOME, WESTERN AUSTRALIA

As the Dakota flew over the Indian Ocean towards Broome, Smirnoff remained on the lookout for Japanese fighter planes. Japan did not want Australia to become a springboard for a US counter-offensive and was considering invasion. Since the bombing of Darwin—with the loss of 243 lives—planes evacuating Allied servicemen and displaced civilians were moved through Broome. In the ten days before Java fell, 8000 Dutch and Allied civilians would be airlifted off the island, with most passing through the once-remote town. Despite unreliable communications, Broome became one of the most vital Allied operational centres in the Pacific War.

When Smirnoff had landed in Broome on his last evacuation run five days earlier, the pearling village had seemed a world away from the chaos ripping through Asia, but as the *Pelikaan* neared its planned destination on 3 March, the town would face its darkest hour.

The day after Pearl Harbor was bombed, the local Japanese population of Broome, which outnumbered the Europeans, had been interned. It was a disaster for the livelihood of the town, which relied on the skill and experience of the Japanese pearl divers and lugger crews. For the rest of Australia it was easy to hate a distant enemy, but in Broome the Japanese had been an integral part of life for half a century.

They could have sailed off in the luggers but they chose not to, making no trouble as they were quietly rounded up and taken to the jail. The luggers were pulled ashore for the lay-up season. Most would never sail or see the pearling grounds again.

By February the whole north coast of Australia feared imminent invasion and local women and children were evacuated south—but not all agreed to go. Biddy Bardwell operated the Broome telephone exchange and post office. When Inspector Cowie, the local police chief, had impressed upon her the need to leave, she told him in no uncertain terms that if he thought that she, Marjorie Bardwell, would let herself be shipped out of town 'like a common refugee', he had better think again.

Her husband, Beresford, a pearler immortalised by author Ion Idriess in his Australian classic *Forty Fathoms Deep*, also urged her to join the rest of the women leaving town, but again she refused, saying, 'I am not fleeing from a bomb that has

"Made in Japan" stamped on it. Who will take care of the telephone exchange? Get it into your head, Beresford—Marjorie Bardwell is staying in Broome!' And that was that.

On the jetty that ran into Roebuck Bay, Biddy had joined the remaining men in the town farewelling their wives, friends and children. Biddy wept as her best friend, Margaret De Castilla, boarded the boat for Perth. Margaret's husband, Jock, had clutched their tiny baby tightly in his arms, distraught at the prospect of being separated, until it was time for mother and baby to board the MV *Koolinda*.

Many of the residents had convinced themselves the ship would be torpedoed or bombed before it reached Port Hedland, and not without reason. Rumours had reached town that the *Koolinda*'s sister ship, the *Koolama*, had been bombed by Japanese planes. The ship was missing and its fate unknown. Nevertheless, the *Koolinda* steamed out of Broome with sixty-three women and sixty children on board on 27 February—the same day the Japanese attacked the Allied fleet in the Java Sea.

Jock De Castilla had heard the rumours about the bombing of the *Koolama* and hoped the *Koolinda*, with his wife and baby on board, would make it to Perth safely. As manager of the pearling fleet belonging to Gregory & Co, Jock's work on the luggers had almost come to a standstill in the last few months. The only luggers now in use were being deployed to help refuel the many flying boats coming into the harbour, their numbers growing each day. Gregory & Co had a licence with the Vacuum Oil Company, which supplied fuel for Broome. The fuel was now needed for the massive influx of aircraft landing in Broome in the ferrying operation between Java and the Australian eastern states. Roebuck Bay was an excellent harbour for flying boats. The canvas sails of the pearling luggers that once filled the horizon were replaced by the large flying boats which skimmed the surface like seabirds, floating, bobbing on the waves, waiting for fuel, before taking off again into the blue sky. With as many as fifty aircraft arriving daily to refuel and leaving as fast as they could, Jock's pearling luggers were kept busy taking drums of fuel out to them.

Vacuum Oil also supplied fuel for the land-based aircraft using the airport. The Broome landing field was capable of taking the largest aircraft, and Allied intelligence believed Broome was out of the range of Japanese aircraft. Besides, the Japanese seemed to be concentrating all their efforts on capturing Java.

Colonel Richard A. Legg, USAAF, arrived in Broome to organise the evacuation of the American personnel from Java on 1 March. One US Army staff officer remarked that Broome airport was the busiest he had seen outside the United States, writing in his diary, 'The place looks like La Guardia Field. Entire small 'drome now covered with ships. Men sleeping on floors, porches or any other shelter they can find...'

On the morning Smirnoff was due to arrive in Broome, dozens of land-based aircraft and flying boats flew in ahead of him.

No one had been prepared for the massive influx that morning. Qantas had a tender to ferry the crews of their flying boats ashore, but no such arrangements had been made to ferry the crews or passengers of the Dutch flying boats. A single fuel-laden pearling lugger, the *Nicol Bay*, headed across the water to refuel the Qantas flying boats. The larger Dutch Dornier aircraft would take forty minutes to refuel. It would be a long stopover.

The night before, some of the Dutch Dornier commanders had asked permission to leave, as their aircraft had been refuelled, but they were ordered to remain until morning to get some much-needed rest. Most of the crews had been on duty for days on end, operating the shuttle service between Java and Broome, and they were utterly exhausted.

Unfortunately for many of the passengers, lack of accommodation in Broome meant they were forced to wait on board the aircraft while the captains sorted the paperwork and rested onshore. Adding to the delays, the eight-metre tides of Roebuck Bay made ship-to-shore ferrying difficult. The far north is notorious for its huge tides and March is when the tides vary most dramatically. On the morning of 3 March, the low tide was enough to hamper the movement of the aircraft and support boats, and some flying boats were stranded in the sand, the refuelling boat unable to reach them. The planes planned to move on, mostly to Perth or Sydney, as soon as they were refuelled and the water rose high enough under their floats to enable a safe take-off. Flying boats continued to arrive throughout the early morning.

On board Dutch Catalina X67, navigator Henri Juta filled out his log and looked up at the weary, forlorn faces of the passengers. The only one of the thirty-three passengers he knew was his wife, who sat in a corner by the radio equipment gazing at her husband, her face full of fear. 'We're fine, love. We've landed on the water and nothing can happen now,' he reassured her.

For a moment there was relief and everyone started talking. Juta opened the hatch above the chart table and climbed out of the aircraft. The heat rising from the metal surface of the plane hit him, but also the wonderful fragrance of the desert and the sea. In the distance he could see the outline of the jetty and he watched as more flying boats landed on the bay. Inside the plane, the women busied themselves preparing food and making coffee. The radio operator was annoyed at other aircraft using their radios to contact Java. 'With all this noise we may as well just tell the Japs we're here!' he shouted angrily. He wanted to get moving and handed Juta a megaphone to try to make contact with the shore, but they were too far away and it seemed that everyone in the town was asleep. It was 7.15 a.m.

The metal hulls of the flying boats held the tropical heat like ovens. Women, men and children were cramped together in the small cabin with nowhere to stretch their legs or breathe fresh air, let alone sleep. Weary children whined as their mothers lamented their lost homes. Still, this was war, and at least they were alive. The adults had secured precious space on these planes for which air service personnel vital to the war effort had first preference. There was little doubt in their minds that their friends and families left behind in Java were in a far worse position than they were.

But as the heat built up the atmosphere in the Catalina began deteriorating fast. All the windows and blisters were opened and three double 7.7 mm guns were turned outside to make space so the passengers could sit on the barrels. Juta urged his wife outside into the fresh air as she was suffering from seasickness, but she did not want to move. A twelve-year-old boy, Robert Lacomble, joined Juta; his father, a commander on the flagship of the Dutch fleet, the light cruiser *De Ruyter,* had died four days earlier when the ship was sunk by Japanese torpedoes during the Battle of the Java Sea. Fascinated by the flying boat, Robert asked an endless round of questions about the Catalina. Juta pointed out another flying boat coming into land and the boy watched excitedly as the huge, high-winged Dornier Do.24K with its 27-metre wingspan skimmed across the surface and came to a halt.

Henk Hasselo had never flown a Dornier float plane when he was assigned to co-pilot Dornier X-1 to Broome the night before. The normal complement for the X-1 was a crew of seven, but on this trip they had carried between forty and forty-five people.

Instead of floats, the Dornier had sponsons which protruded from the sides of the craft like low wings. The sponson was similar to a float in that it was designed to stabilise the craft when it was moored in rough seas and keep it from tipping over. Right now, they also provided a platform to which people could escape from the cramped, smelly cabin. A few excited children were running in circles over the sponsons, glad to be outside. Adults were assigned to watch them for fear one might slip into the water and drown.

Henk Hasselo climbed through the hatch onto the top of the Dornier. The massive wings of the flying boat were held up high above the body of the plane by metal supports which ran from both the body of the plane and the sponsons. Hasselo had a good view of the harbour from the top and was shaded from the sun by the wings overhead. There was no ventilation in the hot, overcrowded aircraft and he was glad to be out in the fresh air. He scanned the harbour for a boat that could ferry the crew to shore to organise paperwork and refuelling, but there was none in sight.

He could see a tiny seaplane dwarfed among the huge flying boats. The Curtiss SOC Seagull float plane had been assigned to the USS *Houston*, the flagship of the Asiatic Fleet sunk by the Japanese in the Battle of the Java Sea. When the *Houston*'s two other float planes were shot down, the captain ordered the pilot to fly south and save himself if he could. Broome was

800 kilometres away and he made it on the last drop of fuel. With his plane now refuelled, he taxied across the water eager to depart ahead of the big flying boats.

At the end of the Broome jetty, passengers and crew from the Qantas flying boat *Corinna* waited for dinghies to take them back to the aircraft ready for take-off. Also on the jetty were the crew from the British 205 Squadron Catalina FV-W, who had been evacuated from Java and arrived the night before. Another British Catalina, FV-N, arrived around 9 a.m.

'Another Cat,' Robert shouted to Juta, clearly excited by his new-found knowledge of flying boats. There were now eight Catalinas on the bay: four Dutch, two belonging to the United States Navy and two British. The fiancée of the second pilot climbed through the hatch, joining Juta and the boy on the body of the plane. Inside, many of the passengers had become seasick and the stench of vomit in the hot, humid cabin was overwhelming. Juta went inside and eased his wife outside, where she started to feel better.

Robert continued questioning the navigator. 'Sir, what is that strange thing sticking out of the side of the plane?' Juta started to answer, 'It's a—' but he didn't finish his sentence. A low droning noise that was getting louder drew their gaze skywards.

The fighter planes came in above the lighthouse at Gantheaume Point which guarded the mouth to the bay. At first Juta thought they were Australian RAAF planes and the boy was about to wave when the second pilot said something about a gun. The planes peeled away and they saw the telltale red rising sun on their sides.

At 7.05 a.m., nine Zero fighters and a C5M.2 'Babs' reconnaissance aircraft under the overall command of Lieutenant Zenziro Miyano had taken off from Kupang in Timor, headed for Broome. Simultaneously, Commander Takeo Shibata ordered a further eight Zeroes to attack military targets at the northern Australian port of Wyndham. The Mitsubishi A6M Zero fighter plane was a masterpiece of aviation. Its long-range capabilities and manoeuvrability brought astounding victories to the Japanese in the early days of the Pacific war and made it a legend in its own time. With it, the Japanese had decimated the Allied forces, and the sight of the aircraft now brought terror to the hearts of the onlookers.

The slim silver fighters jettisoned their auxiliary belly tanks, which held the fuel that had enabled them to make the distance from Timor to Broome. To the onlookers below, the tanks plunging through the sky looked like bombs. The Zeroes then took up attack formation—three flights of three—and began to close in on their targets sitting helpless on the water. Within seconds, red bursts of gun fire sent white plumes racing across the surface of the bay.

The Australian Qantas flying boat *Centaurus*, a Short Empire A18-10, was the first to explode and sink. Captain Caldwell and his co-pilot had spent the night ashore. As the plane burned the crew threw themselves into action. One man rushed to the flight deck as bullets exploded around him, grabbing an inflatable dinghy and flinging it out the door into the sea. The remainder of the crew dived through the hatches, jumping into the water after the dinghy. Miraculously, all escaped and set about rescuing survivors.

The Zeroes were fitted with two cannons in the wings, each containing sixty rounds of heavy 20 mm shells, plus two centrally mounted machine guns. The cannon shells were fired first, causing most of the devastation and destruction.

Instinctively, Juta shoved his wife from the plane into the water and then pushed Robert into the bay too. Juta jumped in after them, taking the fiancée of the second pilot with him.

Nearby he saw the tracers dance like fairy lights towards their target. The tracer bullets held pyrotechnic chemical flares in their hollow backs, which allowed the pilot to see where his bullets were going without looking through a gun sight. The Zero pilots 'walked' their cone of fire towards the Catalina using the tracers as a guide. As Juta later recalled:

We disappeared under water and when we emerged about two seconds later the world had changed. There was lead, fire, blood, death and ruin. The Cat was alight and the young woman was hanging on a support between the wings and the bulk of the plane. She yelled, 'I'm hit!' Blood poured from her face and the water below her was turning red. All I could think of was my wife and I swirled in the water to find her.

I saw her just a few metres away; her black hair clinging to her face. She called my name. I swam to her and she clung to me. It was all I could do to keep myself above the water. 'I can't swim like this,' I told her and I managed to get her to hold on to my shoulder. Just then I saw that a Zero was opening fire again. 'Duck!' I yelled to my wife and we both managed to get under water. We were not hit so I just thought I was lucky. Later I learned that the Japs shot in the water with machine guns and just before they came to the target they would shoot with a 20 mm cannon.

Rising to the surface I witnessed a shocking scene. A man jumped down from the plane with a small child in his arms. He called to me, 'Help, help, I can't swim anymore.' A few seconds later he disappeared under water with the child still in his arms.

Sergeant P. [probably C. van der Plas] swam to his fiancée but she was already dead. Her face was full of bullet holes. There was another attack and I had to pull my wife under again. When we surfaced we saw a small boy come out the hatch and a woman jumped after him. They disappeared at the other side of the plane. The Cat was sinking fast. Smoke and flames were coming out of the hull. The last I saw of the sinking ship was Mrs Lacomble [the mother of Robert], trying to climb out of the hatch. I think her clothes were stuck in the barrel of the double-barrelled gun. She disappeared later, together with the tail end of the plane, screaming and struggling under water.

My wife and my own situation needed my full attention now. She had swallowed a lot of water and she was coughing and clinging to my shoulders. I began swimming but my strokes were too fast and irregular. As a good swimmer I realised I was doing it all wrong, but at that moment it was the only way to stay afloat. I was fully dressed in shirts and shorts, woollen socks and sturdy shoes. I also had a gun attached to my belt. The most uncomfortable were my woollen socks and the shoes, and my legs felt like lead. I tried to kick off my shoes but my wife, who was clinging to me, weighed me down and I almost drowned. All around me there was an inferno of fire, explosions and screaming people who were dying.

The Zeroes peeled downwards like seabirds diving for fish, picking off one refugee-laden plane and then moving on to the next.

On Henk Hasselo's Dornier, all those inside the cabin pushed towards the door. Bullets ripped through the fuselage and people were shot as they tried to flee. Gun fire, smoke, screaming and shouting filled the air as those who could get out leapt into the water. Hasselo, still up the top, ran towards the gun turret at the tail of his plane. There was an entrance to the turret from the outside. He opened the hatch and jumped in. Poking his head out, he spotted the planes above and was able to fire off a few rounds at the Zeroes. A few bullets found their mark, but they weren't enough to stop the attackers. The sponson on the left was so badly shot up that the Dornier tilted to starboard and started to take water. There were still people trapped inside. A thick pall of smoke surrounded the plane and Hasselo couldn't see to shoot anymore, so he too jumped into the sea.

From the plane, Jan Piers and Simon Koens, both trained marines, leapt into the water, as did Simon's wife Sara and their son Piet. Simon's eleven-year-old daughter, Elly, heard her father calling for her to jump in, so she sat down on the sponson to take her shoes off as she always did before she went for a swim. Now she could hear the voice of her mother, Sara, pleading, 'Jump, Elly! Just jump!' Elly stood on the wing and looked down at the water. 'Is it cold?' she called out. Her father was drifting away with the powerful tide; she could see he was bleeding on the face and arm and it worried her. Her mother was trying to swim against the tide nearby, watching as the Zero swept down on the Dornier. Elly jumped into the water, swimming towards her mother, and as she did so she heard screams from the plane. She turned to see Mrs Piers, clinging to the wing supports, screaming 'I can't swim! Help us! I can't swim!' Mrs Piers's seven-year-old son Frans gripped his mother's neck fiercely, while her eleven-year-old son, Cornelius, also held on to his mother. Jan Piers was by now too far away to get back to the plane to help his wife and children. Elly's mother, Sara, was closer but the tide also defeated her and she had no hope of reaching them. Frans began to cry. With bullets flying around them, Elly ducked as Cornelius found the courage to jump. It was too late; he was hit by a bullet and never surfaced.

Elly rose to see Mrs Piers and her little boy shot repeatedly as the plane burned around them. Her mother told her to not look back and to swim with Piet as fast as she could towards the shore. The fuel on the water erupted into a ball of flame as the fire spread rapidly across the bay. Elly, Piet and Sara swam desperately against the tide, trying to escape the pull. Sara was glad for all the times she had taken her children swimming in the mountain lakes of Java and at the local swimming pool.

Jan Piers watched as the Dornier shuddered and jerked at its mooring before exploding into a blaze of light on the water. He had watched as Cornelius disappeared beneath the surface. He had seen the bullets pierce his wife and son and the flames engulf them. The flames leapt into the air in red and yellow streaks, and then there was another roar and three more flying boats went up, fuel tanks exploding and sending burning fuel across the surface as all over the bay figures leapt into the cauldron-like sea. Jan swam on towards shore and made it to safety, but he would never forget that moment. For his split-second decision to jump in a moment of terror instead of staying to help his family, he would never forgive himself.

Tentacles wrapped around Elly Koens's body and she screamed at the pain. Sara tried to pull them off but found herself entangled in the stinging tentacles of what was possibly a box jellyfish. Fear drove them to swim on in spite of the pain. The few boats they could see in the distance were taking the most badly burned people first. The smoking skeleton of the X-1 was some distance away now. Finally a man rowed towards the mother and daughter. Hauling them up into the dinghy, he turned and took them back to shore.

The Zeroes wove mercilessly in and out of the dense smoke that saturated the bay. Appalled pilots and crews watched the carnage helplessly from the shore, numbed as their aircraft and passengers burned.

Inside Catalina Y-59, Sophia van Tour stared in horror as a bullet struck her twelve-year-old daughter Catherina in the eye. Her husband Albert grabbed the screaming child and pushed Sophia out the door with a lifebelt. He followed Sophia into the water, holding his bloodied daughter. Sophia was unable to swim but floated with the aid of the lifebelt while her husband swam nearby, trying to keep Catherina afloat. They were drifting apart and Sophia watched helplessly as he suddenly disappeared beneath the surface, still clutching their daughter.

Nine-year-old Catharina Komen-Blommert stood stunned as her father crumpled before her, killed by a bullet. She was pinned to the floor of the aircraft and filled with terror. Someone lifted her up and tossed her into the water, but she couldn't swim. She splashed about, struggling to keep afloat. A wounded man, seeing her, swam back and grabbed her around the waist, trying to calm her down, encouraging her to float. Suddenly he let go, slipping beneath the surface, and she was on her own again. The wounded man had used every ounce of his strength trying to keep Catharina afloat. There was another loud roar and then the sound of women screaming. The rear of the plane was gutted by fire and sank at anchor. The bullets continued to strike the water around the terrified child as the strafing went on from above. She felt herself sinking, spitting out mouthfuls of water. Luckily, one of the Australians from the *Centaurus* spotted the struggling child and rowed up to her, pulling her to safety.

At the first sound of gun fire, Bart van Emmerik urged his wife Frederika to lie down with their baby, Bernhard, and he lay on top of them to shield them from the bullets. When Frederika spoke to her husband, he answered very slowly and was panting heavily. Frederika knew he'd been hit. Again she spoke to him, but this time he didn't answer. His full weight now rested on her small frame. She tried to move, and on turning her head saw that her own arm had been shredded by bullets or shrapnel. In panic, she pushed the body of her husband away and dashed for the exit. As she leapt into the water, she turned in horror to see the plane's mechanic, Sergeant Brandenburg, clinging to the port sea-anchor rope, shouting for help. Within seconds the petrol tank burst into flames. Brandenburg and the surrounding water became an inferno and Frederika swam desperately to escape the burning oil. Her baby was still inside the plane with her dead husband.

Lance Corporal Bowden, on board British Catalina FV-N, went to return fire, but a Dutch woman who had rowed out to the aircraft and begged to come on board at Tjilitjap back in Java was frozen with fear against the ammunition pans. Three men picked her up and threw her into the water. Before Bowden could cock the guns and release the safety catches the boat was on fire. He ran to get a life jacket as he couldn't swim, but other crew members trying to get out grabbed him and threw him overboard. Bowden's heavy flying boots weighed him down like a lead sinker. Rolling himself into a ball he pulled off the boots and headed for the surface, gasping for air. He had been hit and his nose and arm were bleeding profusely. Seeing Bowden struggling, two crew members came to his aid, removing his clothes. Convinced he was going to drown, he prayed for help. He had never believed in God before, but found that suddenly he could swim perfectly well—so well that when the rescuers arrived they could not keep up. Bowden was hauled onto a lugger which had rescued the Dutch woman they had thrown out of the plane when the raid began. A beautiful young girl was also pulled out of the water, but there was nothing they could do; she was already dead. They looked out for more survivors and saw an image that would become etched in their minds forever: three young children floated by face down, locked in a tight embrace. Every person on the lugger wept. Six British pilots and crew aboard the Catalina died in the raid, though others managed to make it to shore despite being shot, including Sergeant Pozzi, who swam the full distance to shore with an arm broken by shrapnel.

The day before, the crew of the flying boat *Corinna* had conducted a ten-hour search for the missing Qantas flying boat

Circe, but had found no trace of the aircraft. The crew had spent the night ashore and were on the jetty getting ready for their departure to Sydney when the Zeroes struck. They watched in horror as the flying boats, including the *Corinna*, were sunk one after the other in rapid succession.

The *Corinna* was being refuelled at the time the raid began from the deck of a former pearling lugger, the *Nicol Bay*, which had on board 180 drums of highly flammable aviation fuel. Standing on the deck surrounded by fuel, lugger captain Harold Mathieson yelled at his engineer Jenkins, who was standing at the wing tank of the *Corinna*, to dive clear of the flying boat. Jenkins dived in, remaining under water for as long as he could. He then hauled himself into an empty lugger dinghy that was floating nearby and, after picking up as many survivors as he could, headed for shore.

With tracer bullets flying around his petrol-laden schooner, Captain Mathieson immediately cast off from the *Corinna*, which was now burning, and set about rescuing survivors in the water. By great good fortune his vessel was not hit.

Henk Hasselo was a strong swimmer and he caught up with a boy aged about nine who was swimming towards the shore. Red-faced, breathless and terrified, he was slowing down, exhausted from fighting the tide that seemed determined to wash him back out into the bay. 'I'll die, I can't swim anymore,' he cried. Hasselo slapped the boy and ordered him to keep swimming, urging him on. He picked up his pace and Hasselo told him to take it easy, and swim more steadily, but eventually the exhausted child slipped under the surface. Hasselo dived down and pulled the boy up, swimming against the tide with the child in one arm. Another man came to help and together they supported the boy as they swam for the shore. It was hard work and they were not making good headway. To their relief, they heard a man with an Australian accent yelling, 'You fellas want to stay here, or what?' Looking up, they saw a smiling face leaning over the side of a pearling lugger. Hasselo pushed the boy towards the back of the boat, where he was helped on board, but Hasselo did not have the strength to pull himself up onto the deck. Next thing, he felt himself being jerked up by the strong hand of Mathieson and thrown down beside a dozen or so survivors.

Captain Lester Brain headed Qantas operations in Broome. When the attack started, he ran to the foreshore and, seeing the carnage unfolding, searched for a means to get out to the injured and drowning refugees. Spotting a lugger dinghy, he tried to drag the heavy wooden clinker-built rowboat towards the water. Malcolm Millar saw him struggling and rushed to help. The two men began paddling out towards the inferno of smoke and flames. Hearing cries for help, they found two Dutch aviators supporting a young woman who was on the verge of collapse; nearby another serviceman supported a baby on his chest. The boat could only hold the woman and baby, so with four other survivors clinging to the sides of the boat the two men rowed to shore. Millar and Brain then returned to rescue others.

Heads were bobbing about in the sea of fire as some brave souls waded into the water, trying to save the hapless victims. Fifteen of the flying boats were now charred hulls. They looked like smoking skeletons. Sharks circled the handful of survivors who had escaped the gun fire and burning fuel.

Henri Juta was still trying to keep his wife afloat when the shooting stopped. A Japanese fighter had flown over very low and he distinctly saw the pilot waving at him. Exhausted, he tried to talk himself into not giving up. He looked around for help, but all he could see was smoke and fire. Wrestling with fatigue, he came across young Robert Lacomble, and swam alongside him. A canteen bottle floated by and Juta grabbed it, passing it to his wife to use as a float. He took off his shoes and socks, held his wife by her head and hair and started to swim to the shore.

Nearby a man clung to a discarded auxiliary tank from one of the Zeroes, but just as Juta reached the tank it sank. Minutes later, the sound of a woman screaming pierced the air and they turned to see a man and woman struggling in the middle of a patch of burning sea that was moving towards them; the woman's hair was on fire. Juta began to swim away from the fire, still holding onto his wife, with Robert swimming at his side. They had been heading directly for the fire—the woman's screams had saved their lives.

After they had been swimming for more than an hour, Juta felt something underfoot which he feared was a shark. He believes he would have drowned then and there had he not heard the sound of a motorboat approaching. A few seconds later, an American serviceman who had commandeered a dinghy and was scouring the bay looking for survivors was pulling them on board. A small girl was lying in the boat. She had been shot in the wrist and her arm lay bloodied by her side. The American told Juta that both her parents were dead as he punched a few holes in a tin of juice and handed it to Juta.

They set about rescuing more victims. There were men and women whose faces had been badly burned and one man whose intestines were visible. When the boat was full they headed back for the jetty. It took twenty minutes. Juta picked up a young girl whose small body lay limp in his arms. He thought she could be dead but he could see no wounds. Placing her on a trolley that had been brought down to the jetty, he lifted her shirt and found two bullet holes in her back that went straight through to her heart. Dazed and shocked, he looked around at all the misery and then he gazed beyond. The sunlight shone across the beautiful bay. Tiny wavelets flickered like sequins on a rippling ocean. Only a few smoke plumes rising in the distance gave a clue to the horror of moments before. 'What insanity!' he thought.

On the shore, dazed survivors were met by locals and soldiers eager to help. Injured survivors were being treated on the beach by the only doctor in town.

Broome was practically defenceless; the Volunteer Defence Corps only numbered sixty or seventy men with a handful of .303 rifles. Biddy Bardwell, one of the last white women left in Broome, was late for work and was looking for her handbag and glasses when she heard the sound of gunshots. At first she thought it was a car backfiring until her Aboriginal house girl, Gladys, rushed in calling, 'War's here, planes with sun on wings.'

They both ran outside and saw smoke rising from the bay and the silver streaks in the sky. She ran to her sister's house to make a phonecall but got no reply. By this time the Japanese were overhead, shooting at the aerodrome. The two women ran for shelter but the first trench they came upon was too narrow for them, so they ran to another. A well-known local by the name of 'Old Charlie' was already there—and so smelly that Biddy ran on to another depression behind some bushes and shrubs. All the locals were heading for air raid shelters, slit trenches or the mangrove swamps.

The Japanese pilots made no attempt to fire on the town itself. They had been instructed to attack military targets only. Having destroyed every flying boat on the water, all of them military transport planes, they now focused on the airstrip.

Gus Winckel had landed at the airstrip minutes before the Japanese appeared over the bay. Passing an American Liberator as it taxied up the runway, his Lockheed Lodestar had headed to the refuelling point. Clambering out, he called on Broome resident Jock De Castilla of Gregory & Co to refuel the aircraft. Looking up and pointing at nine dots in the sky, he had asked Jock if any RAAF manoeuvres were expected that day. Jock shook his head and Winckel urged him to sound the air raid alarm quickly. De Castilla told Winckel not to worry as the Japanese couldn't make it this far south.

Winckel wasn't so sure and decided to fetch a machine gun from his plane just in case. Together with his radio man, he fetched one of the two guns recently installed in the tail, along with about 200 rounds of ammunition. Winckel told his mechanic, Charlie van Tuyn, to take the passengers to a large concrete pipe near the runway. Charlie herded the passengers into the pipe, anxious for his wife and child who had taken off from Java before them in Captain Smirnoff's DC-3. They had not yet landed.

Two US lieutenants had also seen the Zeroes approaching the airfield. Jumping into a jeep, they drove frantically along the strip yelling at the American servicemen to take cover.

An RAAF Lockheed Hudson had taxied to its holding position when the pilot, Wing Commander 'Claude' Lightfoot, realised he had left his codes and maps behind. Turning to his American co-pilot, Sergeant Jim Harkin, Lightfoot asked him to retrieve them from the briefing hut. Harkin retorted, 'You left the bloody things behind, so you go and get them.' The mistake saved their lives.

Lightfoot heard the planes as he was walking back to the briefing hut. He turned to see the Zeroes pounce on an American

Liberator that had just moments earlier left the airstrip. Harkin proposed taking off and his gunner was all for firing from his tail gun position but the wireless operator cut the engines, telling them not to be fools; the Zeroes would make mincemeat out of them. The three men ran for cover and watched from the long grass as the Hudson exploded in a ball of flames.

Pilot Warrant Officer Osamu Kudo was chasing Jack Lamade, the US lieutenant who had only just made it to Broome that morning on his last drop of fuel. He had refuelled and managed to get his small float plane airborne as the attack began. When Kudo saw the American Liberator bomber taking off he banked sharply to the right to chase the larger target. Lamade's seaplane had just had its second lucky escape. It was the only aircraft to make it out of Broome.

The Liberator was carrying wounded men from Java. Bomber pilot Lieutenant Edson Kester was unable to counter Kudo's relentless attack, the Liberator crashing into the sea some ten kilometres off Cable Beach. Broken in two, it floated on the water for a few moments before being swallowed in a swirl of oil-slicked water.

Army Surgeon Captain Charles Stafford of the US Medical Corps, assigned to look after the wounded on the Liberator, broke free from the sinking bomber and tried to help the wounded stay afloat but to no avail—he and most of the others soon slipped beneath the surface. Two of the servicemen, Sergeant Melvin Donaho and Sergeant Willard Beatty managed to get away from the sinking plane, swimming for a gruelling thirty-six hours through shark-infested waters, tidal surges and rips, Donaho battling to keep Beatty from slipping under. Of the thirty-three US servicemen aboard the Liberator, many of whom were sick and wounded, only Donaho and Beatty would make it to shore alive. Beatty died a few days later in a Perth hospital.

Japanese pilot Kudo headed back to the aerodrome, diving down at Gus Winckel's Lodestar. In an interview with Dutch journalist Marianne van Velzen, Winckel described the attack.

> The first time they came over they shot the Lodestar to pieces. I was so mad. My beautiful Lodestar. They came over a second time and I knew how they would fly. I just stood there with the machine gun in my hands on the middle of the tarmac. They must have thought I was crazy. They came over and they flew so low. I could see his face, the pilot. I even saw him smile. Not for long though. I gave him a full burst and he crashed.

The Zero exploded, crashing into the sea, and Kudo was killed. Winckel's arm was badly burnt and he bears lifelong scars as a reminder of the encounter. From that time on he was known in military circles as Wild Bill Winckel.

Six aircraft lay burning on the Broome airstrip as the Japanese headed back to Timor.

◆

The arrow flight of Zeroes caught every aircraft in Broome. It was a huge success. The Japanese had destroyed fifteen flying boats and seven aircraft, including two Liberators and two Flying Fortresses, on the airstrip. They had never expected to find so many planes in Broome on that day, nor would they have been aware that the planes, legitimate military targets, contained civilians. The attack was over in about half an hour, after which the remaining eight Zeroes and the 'Babs' headed north to return to their base at Kupang.

It is unknown how many Dutch citizens lost their lives in the Broome raid. There were no records of how many evacuees were on each plane. No record was kept of those who made it to shore, nor of the wounded who died in hospital, nor of the bodies that washed up in the mangroves. Some of the recovered bodies had been mutilated by sharks and many others drifted away, never to be found. Only thirty bodies were recovered from the flying boats, including the unidentified remains of two Dutch women and five children who were later buried in nameless graves at Perth's Karakatta Cemetery. Historian Mervyn Prime lists the names of fifty-eight Dutch nationals, thirty-two US servicemen, and six members of the British 205 Squadron RAF who lost their lives in the Broome raid, but other refugees who sought to escape on the flights leaving Java might have been trapped in the sinking hulls of the flying boats or disappeared on the tide.

There were no recorded casualties among Australian servicemen or the civilian population of Broome.

Leaving behind carnage, bewilderment, fear and misery, the Japanese squadron was returning triumphantly along the north coast when three of the Zeroes intercepted a Dutch DC-3 approaching the Western Australian coastline near Carnot Bay, some eighty kilometres north of Broome.

Chapter Three

MAROONED

The weather had eased but the high altitude brought freezing temperatures for the passengers on board Smirnoff's Douglas DC-3 Dakota. As the passengers and crew dozed, the captain kept his blue eyes narrowed in concentration, ever watchful at the controls. He refused to rely on automatic pilot, arguing that such a device was designed to react the split second after something happened. To be safe, a pilot must act the split second before.

The sun rose, reflecting myriad colours across the rippled clouds. It was beautiful, but Smirnoff could not enjoy the sight, aware as he was that the aircraft was no longer camouflaged by the dark of night.

An irregular stroke on the horizon emerged, wedged between the pale sky and the blue of the sea. Smirnoff smiled: the coast of Australia—a haven away from the carnage that ripped through his new homeland. Glancing around he noted Maria van Tuyn was still dozing, but the eyes of all other passengers were fixed on the distant coastline.

Sergeant Leon Vanderburg held Maria's little boy, Jo, on his knee in the back of the plane and was pointing out animal shapes in the clouds. The boy was enthusiastically identifying imaginary creatures of his own. Vanderburg had a boyish warm smile with gappy teeth, sticking-out ears and a slightly raised eyebrow which gave him a quizzical, friendly look. Maria van Tuyn awoke and Vanderburg passed the boy to his mother.

Sharper and sharper the coastline emerged until they could clearly see the sands of the beaches and the dunes against the break of the waves. The red of the Kimberley unfolded below, the vast rippled landscape cut with vein-like rivers which wove down to the sandy shores, spilling milky debris into the brilliant waters of the ocean. Reefs and islands lay scattered offshore. Sand, mangrove and mud created abstract patterns along the river deltas and, further down the coast, the land became flatter as the Great Sandy Desert reached out to the sea.

If everything went well, they would be landing in Broome in three quarters of an hour and taking on fuel for the rest of their journey.

Smirnoff saw what looked like smoke on the horizon in the distance around the location of Broome. He turned to the radio operator, who had his earphones on and was listening intently. 'Look at that!'

Muller craned his neck and looked through the cockpit window. The eyes of passengers and crew followed his worried gaze. Even though it was still far away, it was clear from the blossoming cloud of smoke it was an oil fire.

'Is there any signal coming from Broome?' Smirnoff asked Muller.

'The safe signal's on,' Muller replied with a puzzled look on his face. There was a sense of growing uneasiness among the occupants of the plane. Muller requested radio contact with the tower, hoping they would explain why the safe signal was on when there was smoke over the town; there was no answer. It was clear to everyone on board that something was very wrong.

'I don't like it,' Smirnoff muttered, 'I don't like it at all.' He immediately changed course, but it was too late. A shadow overhead confirmed their worst fears. Seconds later, the shattering staccato of machine-gun and cannon fire came out of the blue as the silver fighters dived from above, showering the DC-3 with bullets. The Dakota had flown directly into the path of three top-cover Japanese Zeroes returning from the Broome air raid. Coming in from high altitude, they attacked first from the port side.

Smirnoff yelled, 'Down, down on the floor, everybody. Hold on tight!' A trail of splintering fragments flew from the ceiling near the tail end of the plane, finishing up in a crash of breaking glass in the wireless compartment.

Maria van Tuyn stood up and shouted, 'My baby! My baby!' She was hit in the back by the first barrage and another bullet almost severed her left leg above the knee. She fell with her child. Among the passengers rolling helplessly on the floor was Sergeant Leon Vanderburg, who moments earlier had been showing the little boy shapes in the clouds. He had crawled to the front of the plane behind an empty reserve fuel tank. He reached forward and grabbed the child, holding him under his body as the bullets sprayed along the roof. Several bullets pierced Vanderburg's hip and thigh and one blasted into the boy's foot. The stunned child was silent for a few seconds, then he began to scream hysterically. His mother was crying as the blood from her stomach and leg seeped across the floor.

The other two Zeroes joined in the attack. Diving from behind they strafed as they swept past, firing at the DC-3 again and again. Smirnoff felt a stinging pain in his left arm; seconds later his right arm was hit, and then his thigh. But the one-time fighter pilot who had shot down eleven German planes maintained control and flung the plane into evasive manoeuvres, ducking and weaving the cumbersome unarmed craft away from his attackers. Blood dripped from Smirnoff's elbows as the tracers danced by his window and bullets pierced the fuselage, but he continued to grip the joystick firmly with both hands.

The cockpit windows were shattered and the wind roared through them as the plane filled with acrid smoke. The passengers sheltered as best they could under suitcases and boxes. Dutch pilot Pieter Cramerus, who had escaped the clutches of the Japanese only the day before, later described the seconds that followed as 'the greatest show of flying anybody in the world will ever see'.

Like a swarm of hornets the attackers moved quickly, diving at the plane, continuing the relentless fire. From the cabin the heartrending cries of the wounded rang out. Co-pilot Johan Hoffman shouted to Smirnoff that Maria van Tuyn was dying. Smirnoff said nothing. At that moment, every life on the aircraft lay in his hands.

The port engine burst into flames and Smirnoff knew there was a risk that this fire would spread to the fuel tanks and explode. Equally hazardous was the possibility of a structural failure of the wing. He could not outrun the Zeroes, so their only chance was a hasty beach landing before the plane fell from the sky. Before him lay sand dunes and a narrow strip of beach.

Smirnoff brought the plane down in a tight spiral, pushing the control column forward. With a Zero close on his tail still firing, he plummeted towards the earth then, at the last moment, pulled the nose up no more than sixty metres above the sand dunes, trying to get the aircraft horizontal. Loops of fire enveloped the left engine, threatening to explode the whole aircraft. At Smirnoff's signal, Jo Muller reached forward, pulling on the lever that released the landing gear and activated the brake system. The landing gear was locked into position but the right-hand tyre was hit by a bullet and exploded with a loud bang. The Douglas sideslipped close to the dunes, rolling to a stop, sending the nose into the edge of the surf, at the same time effectively dousing the burning engine. It was a remarkable landing. The Zeroes circled above and then started to strafe the beached plane, tormenting their stricken prey.

Daan Hendriksz and Maria van Tuyn were bleeding badly and were both unconscious. Crawling back through the dim cabin, Captain Smirnoff ordered those who were able to try to get out and under the plane, where the water might offer some protection. They would have to time each exit exactly between the strafing runs of the Zeroes.

In the smoke-filled fuselage, mechanic Joop Blaauw pushed the cabin door open and, for a fraction of a second, stood silhouetted against the opening of the doorway as he waited for the right moment to jump—but there wasn't one. The Zeroes were there again before Blaauw had time to duck. The passengers watched horrified as he crumpled into the sea, one knee completely blown away, the other shattered. Jo Muller tried to pull Blaauw back on board but his legs were like elastic bands, both badly broken, and he slipped into the sea, his face white with shock. Still conscious, he used his hands to stay afloat, ducking under the water when the aircraft returned.

The bullets continued to rip through the fuselage of the Douglas. Leon Vanderburg jumped out after Blaauw, getting safely under the water. When he surfaced, Vanderburg swam for his life in the direction of the beach, but his high flying boots dragged him down, making progress difficult. Again and again he dived down under the water, holding his breath as the Japanese swooped in low, firing relentlessly. Timing was crucial; while the water dramatically slowed the propulsion of the bullets, rising at the wrong second would be fatal. He fell onto the beach only to see bullets kicking up sand centimetres away from him. Miraculously the bullets missed.

Smirnoff tried to leave the plane but fell back, only now aware of the pain of his injuries. Carefully regaining his footing, he waited for the sound of the three Zeroes' engines to dull before sliding down into the water. Unable to swim to shore, he sheltered beneath the tail end of the plane with some of the injured passengers. The blood was drying on his hand so he concluded he was not likely to bleed to death. He did not realise until later that the hot stickiness he felt down one leg was a bleeding wound—he had been shot clean through the thigh.

Maria van Tuyn, Daan Hendriksz and the little boy remained in the plane. Those outside could hear the boy crying but couldn't get to him. The Japanese planes remained above, shooting belt after belt of ammunition. Those agonising minutes when the Zeroes refused to leave seemed like an eternity. Finally they swooped down triumphantly without firing, before disappearing into the sunlight.

The terrified group waited for a while, fearing the return of the planes, but now the only sound they heard was that of the ocean crashing against the shore. Their circumstances were dire—seven of them critically injured, with little food, water or medicine, stranded in a totally deserted location somewhere on the remote Australian coastline, surrounded by the sea on one side and sand dunes backed by inhospitable country on the other.

Of the twelve who had boarded the *Pelikaan* in Java, Maria van Tuyn and Daan Hendriksz were unconscious, Joop Blaauw had had his kneecaps blown off and was moaning in agony, and Smirnoff had been shot in the arms and thigh. Pilot Leon Vanderburg had been shot in the hip, leg and side; Pieter Cramerus had wounds to his head and back, and the baby's foot had been shattered. They desperately needed urgent medical attention but had no hope of getting it. The other five men on board—Dick Brinkman, Hendrick van Romondt, Jo Muller, Johan Hoffman and Heinrick Gerrits—had escaped injury.

Those who could walk carefully moved the wounded to the dunes where there was some shade. Hoffman stayed with Blaauw on the water's edge, as the mechanic wasn't up to being moved. Next to them lay Daan Hendriksz, his body riddled with bullet wounds.

Smirnoff surveyed his surroundings. The beach was narrow, backed by small sand dunes, which were studded in parts by wooded areas, and further along there were mangroves along the water's edge. There was no sign of civilisation in any direction, and Smirnoff had lost his bearings in the aerial chase. His small map gave no clues as to where they were.

It was the hottest time of the year in a place where the daytime temperature year round rarely dipped below 30°C. They were on a beach on one of the most sparsely populated coastlines on Earth under a sun that beat down with stifling intensity, sapping their energy, burning their skin and sucking from their bodies moisture that they were unable to replace.

Within an hour of their lucky escape, the lack of water was felt intensely. Adding to their concerns, the rising tide appeared set to swamp the Dakota, which would cut off the survivors from the much-needed supplies on board. Heinrick Gerrits, Jo Muller and Johan Hoffman volunteered to bring what they could, particularly food and water, to shore.

While they were carting supplies from the plane to the top of the beach, Smirnoff remembered the package that had been given to him on the tarmac at Bandung before he took off: 'Take very good care of it. It has great value.' Unable to do it himself, Smirnoff asked Vanderburg to retrieve the package.

The tide was on the rise and the sea increasingly choppy. After an arduous swim, Vanderburg succeeded in hoisting himself into the plane. The aircraft was filled with smoke from blankets still smouldering on the floor. He located his own suitcase easily then hastily moved towards the front of the plane, using a handkerchief to cover his mouth. But the smoke was so thick that Vanderburg was unable to continue his search; half suffocated and suffering from the bullet wound in his leg, he returned to the exit and jumped into the waves. He struggled back to the beach, where he was again pulled from the water, feeling very sick. He tried to carry the suitcase across the beach to the wooded area in the dunes. The blood from his wounded leg dripped onto the white sand. The pain became excruciating and he collapsed halfway up the dune. Jo Muller helped him over to the shade of the trees. As he sat down, Vanderburg realised that his shorts were stained red with blood and found that the bullet had travelled through his thigh and lodged itself above his knee. He could feel it just beneath the skin. Applying pressure to the wound until the blood flow eased, he bandaged his leg, which was painful and stiff.

Using the parachutes from the aeroplane the men constructed shelters to protect the group from the ferocious heat of the sun. The baby's foot was bandaged; his mother remained unconscious.

Afterwards, one of the strongest of the men who had not been injured, East Indies airline employee Hendrick van Romondt, offered to swim out to the plane to retrieve the captain's satchel and search the cabin for the valuable package. Massive tidal movements created strong currents which pulled van Romondt away from the door of the aircraft and threatened to throw him against the fuselage. He swam against the current, grabbing hold of the doorway; he hoisted himself into the cabin where hours before he had cowered in fear for his life as bullets tore through the roof and walls and cut down his fellow passengers. Waves splashed in through the door and broken cockpit window, dousing the interior, which was still on fire; thick smoke and fumes filled the void. He managed to wade through the water-filled cabin to the front of the plane. Opening the locker beside the captain's seat, he retrieved Smirnoff's satchel and felt around until his hands rested on the water-sodden package. He felt dizzy and nauseous as he lifted it out and could only just make out the wax seals through the thick smoke.

As he turned to leave with the satchel in one hand and the package in the other, van Romondt was overwhelmed by the smoke and fumes. He lost his balance and grabbed hold of a luggage rack to steady himself. The water in the cabin was up to his waist and rising. Van Romondt made it to the door of the aircraft and leapt into the sea. The air was clear and he immediately began to feel a little better. The current was sweeping him away from the shore but he was a strong swimmer and managed to swim against it. He saw the dark shadow of a shark not far away and swam frantically towards the shore. Running up the beach, he fell onto the sand, handing the captain his satchel. It was only then that he realised he must have dropped the package inside the plane.

Vanderburg bound splints to Blaauw's shattered legs then turned his attention to Smirnoff, who was also in dire need of help— pieces of shrapnel protruded from his arms, but removing them was so painful that Vanderburg left them there and wrapped a bandage over them.

After the wounded had been tended to as best as possible the uninjured laid out the supplies—nine litres of water and some cans of meat and fruit. Enough for a day, maybe two; but who could say for how long they would be left on the beach to survive? How could they plan? If the days ran into a week, who here would be left?

In a moderate climate, a man could survive only three days without water—in this unbearable heat the need was far greater. The water would have to be rationed carefully. To last five days, Smirnoff designated each passenger approximately 150 millilitres of water per day, a little over half a cup. To measure it out they used an eyeglass from the first aid kit. The eyeglass resembled a small glass goblet the size of an egg cup. They would receive one eyeglass, equivalent to two tablespoons of water, five times a day. If they were not rescued within five days, they would have little hope of surviving. Finding help was imperative.

The loss of the valuable package was put to the back of Smirnoff's mind as he dealt with the more pressing issues of survival. He had earlier scolded Vanderburg for being concerned about money at such a time—Vanderburg had laid out the contents of his wallet to dry—so when van Romondt told the captain he had dropped the parcel, it didn't seem to matter. Smirnoff would later recall in his memoirs: 'Under such circumstances, the judgment of a person over what is valuable and what is not changes substantially. It occurred to me that the safety of life was much more important than the finding of a parcel. Our energy had to be preserved for more urgent affairs.'

There would be hours of waiting and hoping. He assumed the search for the missing parcel would fill a few of them.

Back in Java, the President of the Javasche Bank was still unaware of the Japanese attack on Smirnoff's DC-3. As the plane's passengers battled to survive in remote country, he cabled the Dutch Trade Commissioner in Australia, Jan van Holst Pellekaan, advising him the package of diamonds was on its way.

Chapter Four

DEATH AND DESPERATION

The Dakota crashed on the same rugged coastline as Australia's most renowned aviator, Charles Kingsford Smith, who became lost while attempting to set a flight record from Sydney to the United Kingdom in his Dutch designed aircraft *Southern Cross* thirteen years earlier. Forced down by heavy storms over the Kimberley, he and his crew landed on a mudflat at the northern end of George Water on the banks of the Glenelg River. The aviator and his crew spent twelve days on the mudflats north of Derby, plagued by mosquitos and sandflies and living on mangrove snails and the baby food that had been part of his cargo, delirious with thirst. Smithy survived that episode and went on to break the UK/Australia flight record later that year, but he disappeared without a trace off the Burmese coast with his co-pilot Tom Pethybridge in 1935 while trying to set a new UK/Australia record in a smaller plane, *The Lady Southern Cross*.

Such were the hazards of flying in those pioneering days, as Smirnoff well knew. Was this flight to be the Turc's finale? Would he, his crew and passengers also be recorded in history as missing without a trace?

From the parachute shelter, Smirnoff looked down to the water's edge. Blaauw and Hendriksz had not been moved due to the extent of their injuries. Blaauw was conscious and in acute pain, lying exposed to the stinging sun. They had only been on the beach for a few hours when Hendriksz passed away. A shallow grave was scooped out in the sand; his body was covered in a blanket, and buried with little ceremony—the task of survival weighed too heavily on the minds of those remaining to allow for long mourning. Hendriksz's premonition had proved right. The flight he had stopped his pregnant wife from boarding at Andir airport would be his last.

Maria van Tuyn regained consciousness momentarily and called for her baby son Jo. Leon Vanderburg was tending to the wounded nearby and he moved beside her. 'He's fine. We've bandaged his foot,' he reassured her. Her eyes watered as she strained to speak. 'Take care of him, please,' she begged. She closed her eyes and drifted back into unconsciousness before Vanderburg had time to bring her the child, who was resting under the trees. She died half an hour later and was buried in the sand beside Daan Hendriksz. Smirnoff tried to remember the words of the Russian Orthodox Church's prayer for the dead. The small child did not understand that his mother was gone and called for her. So fretful was the baby that when he was offered his tiny share of the water, he pushed away the eyeglass, spilling the precious water on the sand. Smirnoff angrily chastised him and then felt ashamed for doing so. When they finally got him to drink he would beg for more, over and over, the little voice pleading 'meer tinke, meer tinke' (more drink) and 'ikke wa wa, ikke wa wa' (me, water) until eventually he would cry himself to sleep, utterly exhausted. Smirnoff wrote in 1947, 'The thing that affected us most was the pleading voice of the child constantly asking for water.'

Of the twelve who left Java, only ten now remained alive. Joop Blaauw, who had been shot as he tried to leave the plane, was also in need of constant care. He was feverish, and he too called constantly for water. The others were still strong, but if rescue did not come soon, they would undoubtedly be sapped of their energy and strength. At least Daan Hendriksz had never woken to know the pain and fear of impending death.

When the tide subsided the plane dried out and the passengers were able to retrieve useful items and search for the package, which they did not find. Those able to scoured their luggage, hoping to find something to ease their thirst or hunger—a drink bottle, a packet of fruit gums—anything to ease the intolerable pain in their parched throats.

Jo Muller, Neef Hoffman and Pieter Cramerus set out soon after the Japanese left to scout the surrounding area. They hoped that they would find signs of life beyond the beach. Planning not to travel far they took no water, hoping to find some along the way. A mangrove swamp emerged before them, but as they tried to work their way around it, the rising tide made crossing impossible. The temptation of finding salvation just around the next clump of trees persuaded them to go on. Walking for hours in the heat of the day took its toll. First their mouths and throats felt dry, and then their heads ached. They tried to suck the dew from the leaves on the bushes but it was brackish, and only increased their thirst. Hoffman had taken his shoes off to cross a tidal creek and had continued barefoot. His feet were burnt and blistered and his head began to spin. He told Muller and Cramerus he could not go on and would need to rest before going back.

Muller and Cramerus returned to camp without him that evening, thirsty, tired and crestfallen. They informed the captain that the terrain was inhospitable, waterless and seemingly impassable. They had not seen a single sign of life and had had to leave Hoffman behind.

A heavy silence fell on all. As Jo Muller recalled in a 1972 interview with Dutch journalist Thom Olink, 'The baby kept screaming and we were trying to organise things. There was moaning and we were trying to... When one of us went to take a look, Maria had died and the baby wasn't getting enough water. I don't know...it was all so confusing. I think...[Muller breaks down] Smirnoff sent me off with Hoffman to find help. It was all bush...it was hopeless. We were dehydrating and we knew there was water at the camp so after a few hours we

[Cramerus and Muller] returned. Smirnoff was not amused. He was angry at us for not trying harder.'

Heinrick Gerrits then agreed to head south on his own. The searing daytime temperature had taken its toll on day one, reaching 40°C, and now, acutely aware of their limited resources, travelling in the heat of the day was ruled out. Hendrick van Romondt offered to join him and the pair set out across the pink sand dunes as the sun softened the colours of the landscape to pastel. Unlike the first sortie, they took with them a few cans of food and a drink bottle full of water. The rest of the men tried to sleep in the sand as a blue moon rose above them.

The night was not a quiet or restful one. Joop Blaauw's moans could be heard over the roar of the ocean and the baby often woke crying. Vanderburg recalled seeing morphine in the first aid box they had recovered from the plane. He had no idea how much morphine to give Blaauw or how to administer it correctly, but knew that if it could help relieve the man's agony it was preferable to his suffering. Vanderburg got hold of the morphine and his hand shook as he nervously injected it into Blaauw's arm. As it seeped through Blaauw's veins the injured man's expression changed—the drug helped alleviate both his pain and his anxiety. Vanderburg stayed with him until he fell asleep.

In the morning Hoffman returned, limping from the burns to the soles of his feet. He had run into the two men who had set out the night before. They had given him water and he had recovered sufficiently in the cool of the night to make his way back to camp.

Muller, the radio operator, retrieved his undamaged radio set and worked feverishly to bring it to life. Even after re-establishing loose connections, the battery had barely a whisper of power. Against the odds, the radio crackled into life. It was only for a moment, but it was long enough for Muller to get a message out: three dots, three dashes, three dots, the SOS code known throughout the world, alongside their last known position. It took two minutes and then the current died and the men sat back to wait, hoping the message had been heard.

The humidity was overwhelming. It was like breathing in hot, thick soup. That afternoon the skies opened up, offering momentary relief—cool, quenching rain. Those who could scrambled to find tins, or improvised sails to try to catch the droplets before they hit the ground and disappeared into the sand and the sea, but no sooner had they gathered up receptacles than the rain stopped and the clouds began to dissipate. It was as if God were teasing them.

An hour after Muller sent out the SOS, a familiar sound was heard in the air, filling the group with hope. Despite injury and fatigue, the men leapt up, running onto the beach like excited schoolchildren, waving their hands in the air. Smirnoff smiled as the sound of the engine came closer and stronger. The SOS message had been received. Looking into the sunlight it was hard to make out the silhouetted plane at first, but they could see that it had a huge wingspan and the wings were elevated on struts, like a 'Vultee' Catalina.

But, inexplicably, the plane flew on. The men were not sure if the plane had spotted them, though they could not imagine that their stranded plane would not have been clearly visible from the air. It seemed to take hours for the plane to return, the black dot in the sky getting larger and louder. As it got closer, the men could see it was larger than the Catalina and had four engines atop its wings, not two. Even before the red sun could be seen, Smirnoff knew the plane was not Dutch, American or Australian—it was a Japanese Kawanishi 'Mavis' flying boat.

Smirnoff yelled, 'Duck for cover' as the thunder of the engines reached a menacing crescendo. Blaauw yelled, 'Don't leave me! I can't move!' Dick Brinkman paused. His instinct was to run, but he surprised himself by dropping to the sand beside Blaauw. A small branch offered them no protection. They lay rigid and exposed on the white sand.

Japanese naval pilot Shigeyasu Yamauchi from the 11th Flying Unit had been patrolling the Indian Ocean from Kupang down the Western Australian coastline when he saw the stranded aircraft. He continued on, but remembered the radio message he had heard being transmitted earlier, and was concerned the group was signalling to Allied fighter aircraft. He returned to the site, hoping to ensure the stranded passengers sent no more radio messages.

Hobbling up the beach towards the dunes as fast as he could, Smirnoff turned to see black bombs plummeting from the sky towards the beleaguered Dakota. One after the other, two 65-kg bombs fell into the water as the plane flew on, only to turn and fly back towards the besieged survivors. Smirnoff covered his ears, waiting for the explosions, but there were none. Two more bombs were released, this time exploding on the beach, sending sand fountains into the air. The drone of the engines moved off into the distance. Those who had sought cover in the bushes in the sand dunes stayed put, fearing the return of the aircraft.

They emerged some time later, remaining constantly on the alert for the possible return of the flying boat or other Japanese aircraft. To their relief, the parachute shelters, which must have been clearly visible from the sky, had been spared. Of the four bombs that fell, not a single one hit the aircraft and no one was injured. But the ordeal only served to add to their anxiety.

As the plane thundered away they were left to gather their thoughts. The Dakota lay on the beach like a stranded whale. It would have mattered little if the bombs had reached their target. Riddled with bullets, and pounded by the waves, the Dakota would soon break up. The radio signal that had seemed like such a breakthrough to the outside world had only brought them tormentors. The unexploded bombs that sat in the water were an ongoing reminder of the danger they were in.

Growth covered the faces of the dishevelled men, and more than one of them was suffering from blistering sunburn. For the healthy, the sea offered some respite, though sharks and stingrays were regularly spotted in the water. The men kept to the shallows, wearily checking around them as they swam. They ventured in at low tide, sheltering under the wing of the plane with the cool wet sand underneath. They did not know it then, but the sea also harboured saltwater crocodiles and the box jellyfish, whose sting contains arguably the deadliest natural poison known.

As the stars filled the night sky, the survivors lay restlessly, deep in thought or tormented by insect bites and the pain of their wounds. They were woken from their reverie by the return of Gerrits and van Romondt, only to learn that they too had failed to find any signs of civilisation. Disheartened, those who could slept.

Smirnoff rested his aching legs and stiff arms and cursed at having to continue the seemingly endless task of waiting, listening to the sound of the waves pounding onto the shore and the buzz of insects. As he lay pondering their fate, he again remembered the small parcel and the urgent voice of the man the night they left. 'Take very good care of it.' He wondered what the carefully packaged wax-sealed parcel contained, persuading himself that it could not have disappeared. If it had fallen into the sea then it could wash up on the shore with the next tide. Perhaps tomorrow he would look.

On the third morning they found Joop Blaauw's body at the edge of the surf. In his fevered anguish the night before, he had torn off his leg splints and crawled across the sand into the sea.

It was a heart-rending sight. The men wearily scooped out another sandy grave on the lonely beach beside those of Maria van Tuyn and Daan Hendriksz. Kneeling in silence, they prayed not just for the souls of the departed, but also for their own.

Sitting around doing nothing was too much to bear and the men planned another expedition. That day, the spears of the sun's rays seemed to pierce them more ferociously than ever. The leaves of the trees hung limp and motionless and the survivors, bathed in sweat, thought of nothing but water.

Smirnoff wondered how long he could maintain any discipline when the desire for thirst overwhelmed his men, destroying their rationality. Would they revert to survival of the fittest? Would the healthy turn on the weak? Unless someone found them soon, eight men and one child would face a slow death. Already the little boy's hysterical pleas for water had turned into a whimper.

Smirnoff's thoughts were broken by van Romondt, who came running towards the group, shouting excitedly, clutching aircraft parts in his hand. 'Water,' he yelled. 'We can make water from the sea!'

At first the others were sceptical, but van Romondt carefully explained how he would build a distiller from parts found on the aeroplane and use petrol to heat the seawater. When the water was heated, the salt, being denser than water vapour, would remain behind while the steam would pass through a pipe into a can where it would condense, providing drinkable water.

A blowlamp and some piping were recovered from the plane and petrol siphoned from the wing tanks. Small sticks were pushed into the sand to hold the piping. A kerosene tin was filled with seawater, one end of the pipe placed above to collect the steam. The blowlamp was filled with fuel, lit and placed under the tin. It required constant pumping to keep the flame burning. The men gathered round as the water slowly came to a boil, watching as the steam rose up into the pipe and finally condensed, dripping down into another kerosene tin.

It was agreed that van Romondt should be the first to try the results of his experiment. He lifted the can, holding it to his cracked lips, tipping it until the liquid trickled into his mouth.

'Is it all right?' Muller asked.

Van Romondt nodded. 'A little salty, but drinkable.' They were all delighted that the contraption actually worked, if only in small measure; the few drops it yielded counted towards their chance of survival. From then on, the blowlamp was kept burning night and day.

The survivors did not realise that the closest settlement was a mission post at Beagle Bay, forty kilometres to the north, and that afternoon, four men were picked to head south for help. Before the Japanese had shot down their plane, Smirnoff had estimated that Broome was only about 100 kilometres to the south. The aerial chase had forced the plane to turn constantly to avoid the attackers, but he reasoned that Broome should be closer than when they sighted the town prior to the attack. He hoped it would take the men only a couple of days to reach their destination. In fact, the group was on the north side of Carnot Bay, approximately 100 kilometres north of Broome. On foot, the bays, inlets and thick scrub would add greatly to that distance and could force an expedition off course towards the no-man's-land of the Great Sandy Desert.

Pieter Cramerus, Jo Muller, Dick Brinkman and Hendrick van Romondt would undertake the third attempt at finding water and civilisation. They were given half the supplies. Smirnoff took each man aside and explained that this trip was their last hope. They should not try to return as there would be little or no supplies left and all would be weaker and more desperate. Muller clearly remembers Smirnoff touching his Luger hand gun as he spoke. 'I don't think he would have shot us, but we realised that we should take him seriously,' Muller told journalist Thom Olink.

'Good luck,' Smirnoff said to each man as he shook his hand. They departed when the rabid heat dulled to a swelter. With their departure, the four remaining men and one child lay quietly watching the passing of day to night; in front of them the graves of their dead companions, and beyond the waves at high tide crashing against the Dakota. Like the survivors, the aircraft had first been struck down by man and was now slowly being pounded by nature. But the plane would last far longer than they would.

On the fourth morning, Smirnoff decided to search the shoreline in case the package had washed up onto the beach.

The others had barely moved and lacked motivation. Smirnoff asked for help but no one volunteered.

'What could be in that package that would be of any value to us?' Gerrits scoffed.

'Even if it were food, it would only prolong our misery,' Vanderburg added, and Hoffman nodded in agreement.

Smirnoff set out alone. Scouring the foamy waterline he noticed large crabs, mussels and other sea creatures. Further on he saw a large black object which turned out to be a pair of binoculars from the aircraft. Some hundreds of metres further on again was a box floating on the waves. The letters on the box had been erased by the sea. The box contained radio parts, but not enough to breathe life into the device they had used previously. There was no sign of the parcel.

Tired out, Smirnoff returned to the shelter and lay down to rest. Before he dozed off, he told Heinrick Gerrits, who was tending the blowlamp, to wake him at the end of the first watch.

Life focused around the distillery. It was at least something positive to do and much work went into attaining a thimbleful of water. As well as the pumping, it was necessary to keep the fuel topped up in the blowlamp to ensure the water stayed on the boil. For the remainder of the group left on the beach, thirst was all-consuming and they hovered around the distiller watching the tiny droplets fall into the can. Dry-mouthed, they waited for the moment when they would be assigned their spoonfuls of the precious liquid, but when it came time to drink, the minuscule offering only increased their desire for more. Night and day the distillery was tended to, the day divided into watches to ensure it kept working.

Long practice caused the captain to wake on time. He looked at his watch. It was past midnight and he wondered why Gerrits had not realised his shift was up. Normally the minutes until the end of the shift were watched closely. Rising softly, Smirnoff caught Gerrits gulping down half a cup of precious water. Furiously he dragged him to his feet, then threw him down in disgust.

'I was just so thirsty.' Gerrits was almost crying.

'We're all thirsty! Now get out of my sight,' Smirnoff growled.

Gerrits scuttled off, finding a place to sleep well away from the group.

There was no point in making a scene, as they all might be dead in a few days, Smirnoff thought. Nobody else tried to cheat. Gerrits later assured Smirnoff it would not happen again but Smirnoff kept him on day watch, where he could keep an eye on him, in case the temptation again proved too great.

Later the next afternoon, an excited cry went up from the beach. Heaving himself up from the shade, Smirnoff limped down to the water's edge to see what all the fuss was about. A black shape sat on the sea between the horizon and the shore. No one was sure who had seen it first, but they hadn't noticed it before. Could it be a ship? One man fired distress rockets into the air while the others hurriedly piled branches together and, pouring petrol over the top, set the scrub alight, sending flames high into the air. Gathering up more branches they worked feverishly in the hope their signal would be seen. But the shape sat unmoving on the sea and the men soon realised that it was just rocks exposed by an exceptionally low tide. Had their situation not seemed so desperate they might have laughed.

Meanwhile, over on the east coast of Australia in her temporary home in Sydney, Margot Linnet had been informed that her husband, Captain Ivan Smirnoff, was dead. The conclusion was inevitable, what with the air raid on Broome and no sign of his Douglas DC-3 for four days. The staff of KLM and the Netherlands East Indies Company made the necessary arrangements. Margot, unable to look upon Ivan's spare suit and shirts, called on his friends to take them away.

The first time that Smirnoff had set eyes on the beautiful actress was at an all-night party in Copenhagen in July 1925. He couldn't speak Danish, nor she Russian or Dutch, and her French and English were worse than his. But he had known from the first time he saw her that she was the one.

His friends assured him that he didn't have a hope; Margot Linnet was the darling of Denmark. She had been in the public eye since she was a baby, when she was the subject of a custody battle between her parents and her foster parents. She was the little sweetheart of every young Dane's dreams. As an actress, she played all the young vivacious leads on the stage and appeared in some of the first silent movies on the big screen. Known and loved all over the country, her pictures appeared on postcards and chocolate boxes.

Smirnoff had practised asking her to dinner in Danish but looked bewildered when Margot replied enthusiastically, in Danish, that she would love to go, and discussed the options. The pilot didn't understand a word. Seeing his confusion, Margot used her acting ability to mime her reply.

On visits to Copenhagen Captain Smirnoff showered the young actress with blood-red Dutch roses, practically living on the Copenhagen run from then on. But Margot kept her suitor at arm's length. Four months after they first met, Smirnoff knocked at her dressing-room door to find Margot melting eye-black in a spoon over a candle by her desk. The air was thick with the languorous heaviness of greasepaint, dusting powder and perfume from the dozens of roses he had sent her. Rows of costumes lined the walls.

'I came to tell you my news,' Ivan said gruffly. 'I am going to get married.'

'Congratulations, darling! Anyone I know?' said Margot as she looked into the mirror, applying her mascara.

Taken aback, he paused for a moment, then swept her up in a hug that lifted her off the floor. 'You're her.' They were married on 23 October 1925.

He had not always been a good husband. When Margot was diagnosed with cancer in 1933 as Smirnoff was preparing to make his record-breaking flight to Batavia, she had never breathed a word of her illness, not wanting to take away his moment of glory. For Margot, it had been nine years in and out of hospital since then. He had not handled her illness as well as he might. He couldn't bear the way cancer robbed her of her life and vitality, yet she had always been there for him and he had never stopped loving her.

That fourth night at Carnot Bay Smirnoff couldn't sleep and, like the small child, was bordering on delirium. He could see his sisters and brothers playing in front of their childhood home in the small ancient town of Vladimir, north-east of Moscow. It was a beautiful summer's day and his friends joined him, fishing rods in hand. Smirnoff's fishing gear was the envy of the village and he proudly showed it off. An old man herding goats shooed the boys off with his cane but they didn't care. Through the woods with dense green fir trees and golden oaks and down into the valley they travelled, where the lake stretched out before them. He felt young and strong. They fished and climbed, whiling away the time until the sun dipped below the trees. With the recklessness of youth they sought to find a shortcut home in the woods in the twilight but became lost. Night fell and they gave up searching for home. They built a fire and listened for wolves and bears, enjoying the freedom their folly had brought—yet at the same time, despite his outward bravado, Smirnoff felt lost and cut off.

Half awake, half asleep, Smirnoff drifted in that no-man's-land between dream and reality. He was alone again, this time

in a ditch with grenades exploding around him. He would be
the only one of the Vladimir contingent still to be fighting a
fortnight after they had been sent in as gun fodder for the
Germans on the Eastern Front. With bayonets fixed they had
been told to take out a strongly guarded hill. The signal to
advance came and, as they dashed forward, the hill burst into
fire, the crackle of machine guns and the whine of bullets
shrieking around them. Through potholes carved by grenades
and over bodies he ran as his friends fell around him. He turned
to see a fixed bayonet beside him. Instinctively, he lunged and
parried as he had been trained to do. There was blood on his
bayonet but he had no time to see if the man was young or
old as another was heading for him. Again he fought off his
enemy, and then turned to the hill. Flattening himself to the
ground, he crawled up with the bullets ripping his tunic. He
never knew who killed the gunners or if they fled, but he knew
his job was to silence the guns, so he set about pulling them
apart one after the other. There were no Germans left on the
hill but now he faced a new hazard. The Russian artillery
had arrived late and were strafing the hill on which he and
his fellow soldiers stood. Only nineteen of the ninety-strong
Vladimir contingent survived and many of those were injured.
Smirnoff was recommended for the Cross of St George.

Another memory came flooding back to block out reality—
he was the leader of a patrol bringing back information on the
complicated zig-zagging enemy line at Lodz, the most mixed-
up battle line on the Russian front. The patrol was caught in

the crossfire and he was shot in the foot. He remembered the sound of the grenades exploding, the pain shooting through his body, lying in a ditch created by the grenade in the biting cold, completely alone. Machine-gun fire rang out in the distance. No one in the world seemed to know he was there.

At the hospital, where he had been taken after crawling crab-like through the mud an agonising inch at a time until he found a Russian trench, he had refused to have his leg taken off. In the months it took him to recover, he gazed out the window at the wood and wire machines that were taking to the skies and promised himself he would fly.

He remembered with joy sitting in the pilot's seat, flying helmet and goggles settled, as he soared above the earth, the sound of his engine like music as he engaged in the sport of battle.

On the afternoon of the fifth day the clouds finally burst, bringing a sudden violent storm. Heavy lightning forced the men to retreat from under the wing of the aircraft, where they had been sheltering from the sun. The sand howled around them, stinging their skin, then the wind died and the rain came. It pelted down hard and heavy but, like the last brief shower, it was over all too quickly. Reinvigorated by the rain, the men tried to drink the brackish water as it ran down from the wings. And then it was still again, the sea singing its eternal song.

The next morning, with the rising sun, the vivid reality of the group's predicament hit as harshly as the bright light. It was their sixth day marooned on one of the most isolated and sparsely populated coastlines in the world. They barely moved from their parachute shelter. There didn't seem any point or need. They had used up their water supplies; now they had only the droplets in the distiller.

The day dragged on agonisingly slowly. There was no wind and no conversation, most choosing to close their eyes and rest to conserve energy. They lay listlessly in the shade, which offered little respite from the searing heat, staring at the dense thunderclouds that teased them with the promise of rain but yielded only spoonfuls instead of the cupfuls they yearned for.

During the day, the baby's condition rapidly deteriorated. He was delirious, his skin flushed and clammy. Smirnoff tried to wet his lips but the fevered child barely had the strength to swallow. His large blue eyes stared into Smirnoff's, frightened and helpless, his breathing shallow and his heartbeat rapid.

Smirnoff kept wetting his lips even when the baby had lapsed into unconsciousness. He had wished that the boy would stop crying and now he wished he would start again, but the small child just lay there unmoving.

Smirnoff couldn't bear waiting. He wanted to get away. He told the others he believed they should leave that evening and let fate be their guide.

But the men lacked the energy and the enthusiasm to do anything. They preferred to place their hope in the four men who had set out three days earlier.

Chapter Five

SURVIVAL

There are only two seasons in the north of Australia: the wet and the dry. Both are hot, but the wet is far hotter, with the temperature reaching as high as 40°C. When the rainy season hits between November and April, the land turns green, and a throng of insects is awakened. Creeks and rivers flood the plains, spilling floodwaters, sand and mud far out into the sea. This outpouring collides with the sway of the tides, changing clear blue waters to a milky turquoise hue close to the shore. Further north waterfalls cascade over rocky outcrops and spill through deep gorges, but on the Dampier Peninsula, where the Great Sandy Desert meets the ocean, there are few waterfalls or gorges, and the land away from the coast is mainly flat and featureless.

In March the rain eases but the humidity doesn't. The air is thick and heavy. The steamy heat has been known to drive

men 'troppo'—a term used by locals to describe a state of irri-
tability bordering on madness.

As Dick Brinkman, Hendrick van Romondt, Jo Muller and
Pieter Cramerus ventured south, starving and dehydrated, their
heads were spinning and tempers frayed. Following the coast,
the only waterfalls were the streams of perspiration that ran
down their faces and necks and soaked their clothes. Mosquito
and sandfly bites covered all exposed areas of their skin.

They were surrounded by vast, open grey swamps that filled
only on a king tide. The mud looked hard and baked on top,
but as they moved across the surface they found themselves
sinking up to their knees in muck the colour of curdled milk.
Trudging on with the mud filling their boots, the group stopped
before a tidal creek which cut their path.

'Look at that,' van Romondt remarked. 'You can see the
water pouring into the stream, and it's rising by the second.'

'We'd better get moving, before it becomes impassable,'
Muller said, pulling off his boots and trousers. He stepped into
the water, surprised by how deep it was. The bottom was soft
and his footsteps stirred up the mud. Pieter Cramerus followed
on behind, carrying his clothes high to keep them dry.

As they crossed, the surging water rose around them and
the three men who had entered the water were soon struggling
against the fast-moving current. Van Romondt had not gone
far and decided to return to the bank where Brinkman still
stood; Muller managed to scramble up the opposite side. Only
Cramerus remained in the water. He was swimming after his

clothes, which had been swept out from under his arm. Unable to reach them, he watched as they disappeared from sight.

Muller pulled Cramerus up onto the bank, but they were now separated from the others by a stream that was still growing in size.

'We'll follow the stream,' van Romondt yelled.

'It's probably best if we separate, anyway,' Cramerus replied. 'We'll have more chance of finding help that way.'

Cramerus and Muller took a more southerly route, waving farewell to Brinkman and van Romondt who headed north, hoping to cross the creek upstream. With only his boxer shorts left to wear, the sand and mud burnt Cramerus's feet and the marauding sandflies and blistering sun tormented his unprotected skin. There was no shade, the going was agonisingly slow, and when they at last emerged onto more solid ground, with low pink and grey coastal heath fringing the swamp, it too was shadeless. The wounds on his head and back, sustained during the attack on the Dakota, throbbed.

Finally, they reached thick, straggly scrub which offered some respite from the sun. They looked back across the swamp but could no longer see Brinkman and van Romondt. The men pushed aside prickly bushes and long grass which scraped against their skin as they moved inland. A large flock of black cockatoos squabbled and screeched in the trees above them and the thrum of insects filled the air.

On the following night they reached a broad arm of the ocean. The silver water stretched out into the distance, cutting their path and reaching deep inland. They did not know the depth of the inlet or if there were sharks and crocodiles in the water. They sat down on the bank, frustrated and exhausted by yet another obstacle. They decided to sleep, planning to find a place to cross upstream in the morning.

The next day, they were pleasantly surprised to find that the water had subsided with the tide and an inlet narrow enough to swim across lay before them. On the other side they ducked around thick scrub, creeks and mangroves. Where they found a path through the bush they would follow it. At best they were covering two or three kilometres an hour, and their resources were rapidly running out.

Ahead on the horizon a glimmer of shining water filled them with hope. Flayed by spear grass, they pushed forward with renewed vigour, but the mirage disappeared to the distant horizon, always just out of reach. The reality of what lay ahead was a dry salt lake.

On that second day they drank their last drop of water, even though they had stuck to their two-tablespoon ration per every three daylight hours.

In Melbourne, a world away from Cramerus and Muller, the package of diamonds had not arrived. The Commonwealth Bank officials and the Dutch trade commissioner became anxious, and fired telegrams back and forth expressing their concerns. A memo urged the bank to take 'all practical steps to trace the parcel'. In Sydney, a two-minute silence was held in memory of Captain Smirnoff.

Termite mounds stood like tombstones in the bush. A thicket of pandanus palms broke the monotony of the woody scrub. As Muller and Cramerus neared it, they saw what looked like water nearby. Another mirage, they told themselves, afraid to get their hopes up. But this time, it was not an illusion; a pool of water lay within inches. Fearing it was salt, Cramerus knelt down and wet his mouth. Looking up at Muller, he smiled through dry, cracked lips. The water was dirty and brown but it was not salty. The clay soil and rocks had held the cool liquid from the clouds above long enough for them to savour it. They jumped into the pool and sat in the water for hours, drinking it up and feeling reborn. Mobs of cockatoos burst through the treetops squawking, as if they found the situation amusing.

Cramerus gazed at the murky water and wondered why it was that each time he was at the end of his tether, staring death in the face, God threw him another lifeline.

Only four days ago, Pieter Cramerus had been captured by Japanese soldiers on Java with his commanding officer, Lieutenant Commander Beckman. Cramerus had been taken by his captors to a tiny village in the countryside which he didn't recognise and marched into a deserted office building two storeys high.

Inside the lobby were chairs where once customers might have waited for service. The morning light streamed in through the window. The room was inoffensive, like a government office or bank. An Australian soldier sat tied to a chair with his head down. His captor pointed at a chair not far from the soldier and Cramerus obediently sat down, allowing the Japanese soldier to tie him to it. Moving outside, Cramerus's guard left the two men sitting in the agonising quiet of fearful contemplation, neither daring to speak, both completely aware of their own desperate plight. The stories Cramerus had previously heard of the horrific torture endured by POWs at the hands of the Japanese played through his mind. He did not know what the Japanese had done with Beckman.

Cramerus was aware of only one guard, although others may have been around. As he fiddled anxiously with the ropes that tied his hands he could hear the guard talking to some local Javanese on the verandah. He wasn't sure what he would do if he could free himself, but anything was worth a try. Finally Cramerus felt the pressure of the ropes ease and loosen until he was able to slip them from his wrists.

He turned to the Australian and asked if he wanted to go, to try to make a run for it. The language barrier didn't help. Looking out the window at the guard, the Australian shook his head; perhaps he considered the Dutchman mad for even trying to escape.

On the porch, the Japanese soldier sat with a sword on his lap, still talking with the group of locals. Cramerus waited until his head was turned away in conversation before slipping quietly and fearfully out the door. The Dutch lieutenant did not turn back to see if the soldier had seen him as he vaulted over the porch railing around the corner, his steps gathering pace until he was running for his life.

He ran past a restaurant where a Javanese man was breaking liquor bottles with a hammer. The crash sounded like bullets and he feared this would draw attention to his escape. About a hundred metres ahead lay a sewer drain and he decided to run towards it. Slipping into the open pipe he continued to run breathlessly through the foul water, the sound of the breaking bottles fading into the distance. Beads of sweat dripped down his forehead. He could feel the adrenalin induced by fear seeping through his veins, his pulse racing as the sound of his boots splashing through the water reverberated through the silence.

After about half an hour Pieter reached the end of the drain, and cautiously hoisted himself up into the deserted street. It was still early morning and the tropical heat had not yet developed its sting. There was no time to stop and think or empty his boots. He knew the Japanese would be pouring over the island like an army of ants, and if they caught him he would suffer a certain and painful death.

He headed out of the town and into the countryside, cautiously ducking behind buildings and trees until he saw a local approaching on a motorcycle and flagged him down. The motorcyclist, a telephone repairman, slowed to a stop as the Dutchman explained the Japanese lay ahead. Warning the

motorcyclist that he too could become captive, he convinced
the man to alter his course and take him back to Bandung,
assuming it had not already fallen. The smelly pilot climbed
on the back of the bike and the two men rode back to Bandung.

The motorcyclist dropped Cramerus outside the palatial Italian
Renaissance-styled government headquarters, the Gedung Sate.
The colonial masterpiece was a unique blend of east and west,
a sprawling whitewashed building with arched verandahs spreading
out either side of the central facade, which was adorned with a
pagoda roof and spire with six bulbs resembling a satay stick.

Reeking of sewage, Pieter Cramerus made his way through
the immaculate garden of the Sate with its manicured hedges
and clipped lawns, through the pillared archway and up the
stone staircase to the reception desk. The officer at the reception
desk eyed the wet, smelly airman with some suspicion as he
pleaded to see the head of government. Finally he was shown
down the long well-lit corridor with soaring ceilings into the
marble- and wood-lined office of Mr Spit, the head of the
executive branch of the Dutch East Indies government. Present
were two other government officials. Cramerus advised them
his commanding officer had been captured but that he had
managed to escape. They wanted to know the exact position
of the invading Japanese forces he had encountered. He warned
them the Japanese were moments away. It was time to brace
for invasion. As they spoke, the sound of Japanese bombs falling
on Bandung resumed. Within days the city would fall.

Pieter Cramerus knew he was lucky to be alive.

Now, lost somewhere in the Australian bush north of Broome, Pieter Cramerus knew he had to find the will to go on. He was tempted to sit in the waterhole and wait, but that wouldn't change their predicament, nor ease the suffering of those still languishing back on the beach. Muller had suggested Cramerus should stay, as he lacked protective clothing, was wounded and covered in blistering sunburn, but Cramerus was determined to continue. He had a strong sense of duty and was never one to complain. Smirnoff had asked him to find help and he did not want to let him down.

It was Saturday afternoon, 7 March. They waited for the heat of the day to ease. Foot pads, possibly cut by cattle, traced a path through the scrub to the north and the two men decided to follow it. The landscape was frustrating in its sameness, a few clumps of bushes and largely deserted terrain, sometimes rocky, sometimes muddy, but always difficult to pass through. At times they wondered if they had come full circle.

They rested occasionally. They had been walking for three days. Heading off before dawn on Sunday they would again watch daybreak over the Australian bush. Passing clumps of pandanus palms and tall red termite mounds they trudged on, concerned that they were wandering too far from the coast. They had followed the only apparent trail they had come across, but it seemed to be taking them northwards. To their knowledge, there was no settlement north. Dense, prickly bushes blocked any possible southerly route, but continuing to head away from Broome seemed suicidal. They knew how empty Australian deserts were, having flown across the vast expanses of the outback, and the idea that they might stray too far from the coast towards the interior of the Great Sandy Desert crossed their minds.

They were considering diverting from the rough track when Muller thought he saw movement in the bushes ahead, some distance away. Probably just a bird or a kangaroo, he thought, but he pointed it out to Cramerus. The bushes moved again. Their feet felt as if they were pinned to the ground as they stared at the moving branches. Emerging from the bushes, a barefoot Aborigine carrying a spear came into full view. A wave of relief swept over them. They moved hastily towards the man, then slowed, frightened they might startle him or that he would be hostile. As they neared him they could see from his expression they had nothing to fear.

'What are you blokes doing out here?' he asked.

Despite their lack of English, exhaustion and dehydration, they spluttered a few garbled words. The Aborigine understood well enough that they were in need of help. He beckoned them to follow.

Guiding the distressed Dutchmen forward, the Aborigine took them to a soak where some other Aborigines were camped. The group looked up, surprised by the visitors. Muller and Cramerus knelt down to drink from the soak and shortly afterwards the man who had found them returned with a kangaroo slung over his shoulder. The women prepared a fire and the kangaroo was soon crackling on the coals.

The animal was pulled apart and handed around among the group. The best parts were given to the two Dutchmen. Cramerus chewed the food slowly, lingering over each mouthful. Even though he was hungry, Cramerus didn't find the meat tasty, but it satisfied the gnawing in his stomach. Muller and Cramerus tried to explain that their plane had crashed and that there were others stranded on the beach. They weren't sure if they had been understood.

The Aborigines pointed out the track the men needed to travel along. The group could see the Dutchmen were weak and disoriented. As soon as Cramerus and Muller had arrived at their camp, the man who had found them had instructed another man to journey on ahead to tell the people at Beagle Bay Mission. Later in the morning, the two weary Dutchmen followed the track towards the mission. They had not gone far when they saw a mule cart approaching.

Chapter Six

BEAGLE BAY RESCUE

On 8 March, as Brother Richard Bessenfelder readied himself for Sunday morning mass, he thought about how much more comfortable he felt in his riding boots and trousers than in the white robe and black sash he had to wear to church. In the Kimberley wilderness, under the stars, he felt at one with the God he had been called to serve. He knew it would be some time before he could return to the saddle, spending months away from the community on horseback tending the cattle and living on damper, stew and tea. War had suspended the thriving business he had helped his superior, Bishop Raible, build up; the income from the cattle trade rivalled and sometimes exceeded pearling on the north-west coast, but now the ships stayed away and there wasn't enough labour to run the meatworks in Broome. Bishop Raible had seen in cattle a chance to make the mission self-sustainable. Expanding their herd to 3400 had allowed the funding of the leprosarium, the school, and the linguistic and anthropological study of the Nyul Nyul people who inhabited the area.

Prior to Bishop Raible's practical hand, Beagle Bay Mission, 120 kilometres north of Broome, had often been on the verge of ruin. A rigid order of monks, known as the French Trappists or Cistercians, had founded the mission in 1890 hoping to evangelise the Aborigines. Banned from eating meat, fish and eggs, and required to wear heavy monastical robes, the monks were expected to work long hours and produce enough food to make the mission self-sufficient. Oppressive heat, floods, disease, isolation, lack of money and the refusal of the locals to be converted to Christian ways led the Trappists to abandon the mission in 1899, and it later passed into the hands of the Society of Catholic Apostolate, a group of German priests and brothers known as the Pallotines.

Together with the Sisters of St John of God, the Pallotines had established Beagle Bay as a model Catholic mission, with its own school, bakery, blacksmiths and brick kiln, as well as dormitories to house the scores of so-called 'half-caste' children taken by force from their families as a result of government policy.

On top of this, between 250 and 350 Aborigines of Broome were evacuated to the Pallotine Mission at Beagle Bay in the month before the Japanese air raid, more than doubling its population. The Sisters of St John of God had refused to be evacuated, insisting they stay on with their charges. No consideration was given to sending Aborigines south, and a plan to send the nuns and native women and children to Geraldton was abandoned through fear of spreading leprosy. Leprosy among Aborigines had reached epidemic proportions in the Kimberley and was then untreatable. A 1941 amendment to the *Native Administration Act 1905–1936* prevented the movement of Aborigines south of the twentieth parallel, commonly referred to as the Leper Line.

A hotchpotch of tents now crowded the grounds of the mission. Aborigines of mixed descent—who had lived independent lives in Broome, including running their own businesses—were seen as troublemakers, and strict rules were enforced, curtailing their freedoms and keeping them in subordination similar to mission Aborigines. Under-resourced and with tension rising between the evacuees and mission Aborigines, the missionaries felt stretched to the limit. The authorities who sent people to their care failed to appreciate that in such a remote location supplies were extremely difficult to come by. Those same authorities, who were happy to entrust the native population to the German missionaries in peacetime, had not displayed the same level of trust at the outbreak of war. When Australia joined Britain in declaring war on Germany in 1939, the seven priests and eight German brothers were jailed initially in Broome, and later in Melbourne. Following an inquiry, two priests and the brothers were paroled back to Beagle Bay, the missionaries of the Sacred Heart stepping in to ensure Beagle Bay survived. The brothers' and priests' movements were monitored by the army, and Warrant Officer Gus Clinch was assigned to the mission to dispel any rumours of espionage.

The air raid on Broome had shaken all at the mission and everyone was living in fear and uncertainty of what lay ahead. It was hard to tell truth from rumour. Panic-stricken Aborigines had greeted Brother Richard in the bush, telling him Broome had been razed, nothing left. He was greatly relieved to learn this story had been an exaggeration, but then again, it was doubtful that this raid would be the last. Some had claimed the Japanese had landed; he hoped this was fiction too.

Cattle charged across the track and escaped through buckled wire fences which needed mending as Brother Richard walked past stone cottages to the parched field where the church lay. Tropical fruit trees lined the perimeter of the vegetable garden which had provided for the full needs of the community until the influx. After mass, the Aboriginal children would go to work in the gardens, supervised by the women.

The tower on the church steeple turned a glowing pink as the rays of the rising sun reflected on the crushed pearlshell surface. It was hard to imagine, in the serenity of the morning light, the chaos in the world beyond. When he had arrived from Germany in 1935, Brother Richard had marvelled at the beautiful 'pearl' church with its magnificent altar decorated with mother-of-pearl shells embedded in the plaster.

Even the words around the tabernacle, *Dominus Meus et Deus Meus* (My Lord and My God) were cut from mother-of-pearl, framed by cowry shells. Completed in 1918, the church was an outstanding and unique work of art in one of the remotest corners of the earth. It soon became a beacon to the raft of nationalities who travelled the coast: Malay, Manilamen, Koepangers, Chinese and Japanese pearlers, the original inhabitants—the Nyul Nyul people and the Bardi from further north—as well as the Irish nuns and German brothers who had come from across the world to be there.

It was shortly after sunrise when the Aborigine sent by the man who had discovered Muller and Cramerus stumbled upon Brother Richard and told him the news. He was unable to tell the Brother exactly where the plane had crashed, but pointed down the track on which the Dutchmen would be travelling.

Brother Richard went to his superior, Bishop Raible, who was meeting with Gus Clinch. Brother Richard passed on the information about the plane crash, and Raible agreed that a search party should be sent out immediately. Clinch offered to join Brother Richard in the search. While Brother Richard organised the rescue team, Bishop Raible drove to Broome to advise the authorities. The RAAF and the Dutch East Indies Airline were contacted to organise an aerial food drop.

The brother organised a mule team with a spring cart within a quarter of an hour of receiving the news. He instructed Beagle

Bay resident Albert Kelly to prepare a second mule team and follow in their tracks. Joe Bernard, a stockman and Aboriginal tracker who knew the area like the back of his hand, rode alongside. Brother Richard prayed he would find survivors as they set out through the rough terrain.

Meanwhile, an Aborigine from the camp was guiding Cramerus and Muller up the track towards the mission. The two Dutchmen were in an extremely distressed state, suffering from dehydration and sunburn; they were barely coherent, disoriented and confused, but the great anxiety suffered from not knowing if they would ever be rescued had dissipated. The long walk seemed less torturous.

When the spring cart came bouncing along the rough track towards them, they knew their ordeal would soon be coming to an end. Cramerus and Muller were overjoyed to see the smiling faces of Brother Richard and Warrant Officer Clinch, though they were too weary to show it.

Cramerus's skin was burnt red raw and blistering from his exposure to the brutality of the intense tropical sun. Brother Richard cooked up some soap into a paste and caked this onto the sunburn, which offered some relief. Cramerus and Muller were fed and watered and directed towards the mission.

After repeated questioning by Brother Richard and Clinch, the two men were able to draw a few familiar landmarks that gave the Beagle Bay team the clues needed to pinpoint the crash site. Brother Richard and Clinch surmised that the wrecked plane must lie between two certain points. Their carts could not make it through the mangroves, swamps and sand of the coast, so Joe Bernard rode south on a mule in search of the survivors, agreeing to rendezvous afterwards with Brother Richard and Clinch at Bunda Bunda mustering camp, a little over forty kilometres south of Beagle Bay. About halfway to the mustering camp they noticed a low-flying aircraft heading north—possibly also searching for survivors. Within a few kilometres of the mustering camp, Clinch and Brother Richard met up with the other two men who had been sent on the exploratory mission, van Romondt and Brinkman. The two men had become dis-orientated and were heading back along the track towards the crash site. Clinch and Brother Richard fed the two Dutchmen and took them to the mustering camp, questioning them further on the exact whereabouts of the crash. There they waited— both for Joe Bernard, who had travelled on horseback towards the coast, and for Albert Kelly and the second mule team.

The survivors at Carnot Bay lay motionless on the beach. That afternoon, the same ominous sound that had brought fear to their hearts just a few days earlier rose above the sound of the ocean—the unmistakeable drone of approaching aircraft. Soon two black dots appeared in the distance, flying very low in their direction. The planes weaved continuously from left to right as if they were searching. The group of exhausted men sprang into action. They did not intend to play target again. Instinctively they hid themselves in the bushes, pulses racing, anxiously awaiting the sound of gun fire.

Leon Vanderburg removed his white singlet for fear of being spotted and crouched face down beneath a large branch on the water's edge. The planes circled as Vanderburg remembered how the water had protected him from bullets five days earlier. Now, as the planes approached he ducked under the surface and held his breath. Hoffman, Smirnoff and Gerrits were too far away to get to the water and had to rely on surrounding shrubbery to hide behind.

Eventually Vanderburg put his head up to breathe. At that moment, a plane passed immediately overhead and he saw clearly the red, white and blue circles at the ends of the wings. Smirnoff and the other men saw them too. It was the Royal Australian Air Force—they had been saved. Their pain dissipated as Smirnoff, Hoffman, Vanderburg and Gerrits leapt to their feet. Circling low over the beach, the pilots saw a frenzy of waving arms below them. Letters and packages fell through the air. The first short note read, 'Help expedition of the mission post will be arriving at sunset.' The second had more detail— 'The rescue group will be with you tonight with food and medical aid, much luck. Macdonald RAAF'—and the third brought a smile to their faces: 'Good luck and may the Japs rot in hell!' The planes circled above and the men clearly saw their occupants wave before they left.

Adrenalin surged through their weakened bodies. The four men dragged the packages up to the shelter and then tore them open like children unwrapping presents at Christmas, gasping at their contents—water, fruit, meat, chocolate, coffee and even tobacco. It was a feast. Each man savoured the fluid inside the tins. Never had a drink tasted so good. Drawing back on their cigarettes and lying back in the sand, Hoffman reread the messages aloud and they all smiled. Smirnoff found it hard to believe that their ordeal would soon be over.

Thoughts fell to the little boy and Vanderburg walked over to where the baby had been left to rest away from the group. As he neared he saw the child lying curled up under a tree in a clear sandy patch, his small thumb near his open mouth, the bandage on his foot black and red with blood and dust, his eyes closed. Peace had come with death. The rescue party would be too late to save Jo van Tuyn. Shocked, Vanderburg sat down and looked at the child, berating himself for not caring for him better. Had he died in the minutes before the planes appeared in the sky, Vanderburg wondered, or had they been so consumed in indulging their own desperate need that the time taken enjoying the packages' contents had cost the child his life?

Smirnoff, who in the preceding days had tried so hard to get the child to drink, soon joined Vanderburg and was moved to tears. The pilot gathered up the tiny body and wrapped it in a parachute. Holding the child tenderly in stiff aching arms, he limped down to the shore and tried to remember which grave was Jo's mother's. Scooping out a tiny hollow, he lay the baby down and covered him with sand. The other three men joined Smirnoff and they all knelt silently by the grave.

The afternoon sky took on a strange neon-yellow hue as the fire of the sun sank towards the horizon. The men found themselves gazing out across the ocean, drawing back on tobacco, battling conflicting feelings of relief at their impending rescue and dismay at the loss of the little boy. They did not see the shadow glide noiselessly towards them in the twilight. Hoffman jumped up with a yell. None of the survivors had ever seen an Aborigine before and they were alarmed, but the man smiled sympathetically and gestured at them to stay calm. In broken English, Joe Bernard told the group that others were on their way to help, then he went back to the Bunda Bunda rendezvous to report their location.

Clinch and Brother Richard filled water bags and set off on foot with Joe. They instructed Albert to follow with a mule cart as far as the tidal flats and soft sandy beaches would allow it to travel. No foot journey was easy through this harsh terrain but the group managed to make good time, despite travelling through the dark of night, and hindered by cloud moving across the moon. They arrived at the beach at around 2 a.m., to be greeted by the overwhelming stench of rotting bodies, made more pronounced by the still-hot weather. As the smell became stronger they could make out the silhouette of the plane on the beach in the moonlight. They were in the right place.

Brother Richard leant over the sleeping shape of Captain Smirnoff and shook him gently. Half awake, Smirnoff heard the brother's German accent and reached for his pistol, but the missionary reassured the captain and his fellow survivors of his good intention.

Using aviation fuel poured on to the sand and set alight, the rescuers boiled a billy and the survivors enjoyed their first cup of tea in a long time. Brother Richard listened quietly as the men recounted their ordeal. In the firelight he could see the trauma in the faces of the weary men as they told of the attack, of the mother and child who now lay buried on the beach, of the anguish of the pilot who had left his pregnant young wife behind, of the agonised screams of the young mechanic who lay for days on the beach, his kneecaps blasted away.

Warrant Officer Clinch walked down to look at the graves on the beach. The whitecaps of the waves rippled on to the shore. As he gazed at the four mounds, Smirnoff limped up behind him and pointed at the smallest one. 'The little boy. He died only a few hours ago,' he said. The wind had blown a top layer of sand away and another storm would leave the bodies fully exposed to the elements. They would need to be reburied.

The rescue party were weary from their long trek but there was nothing on this shore that made any of them want to stay, and Brother Richard could see the survivors were in dire need of medical attention.

Smirnoff told Clinch of the valuable package he had been given as he prepared for take-off from Java, but it seemed insignificant now, with the pain of death still weighing heavily on their shoulders. There was neither time nor inclination to

search for it—if the men wanted to get out, they would need
to use the cool of the morning. Clinch offered to return the
next day with a group from the mission to search for the package
and bury the dead.

'Can your party walk?' Clinch asked. Smirnoff's heart sank;
three of the four survivors had serious leg, foot and hip injuries
that would make walking any distance extremely difficult. 'It's
a good mile or two, nothing but foot tracks through the scrub;
we could not bring the horses nearer,' Clinch continued.

Smirnoff nodded. At four o'clock on Monday morning they
set out in single file, guided by men who knew the rugged
terrain well in spite of the sparse light from the shrouded moon.
Heavy mud and uneven ground ensured that every step would
be felt by the wounded. Vanderburg used a branch to help
support himself, but before long the wound above his knee
where the bullet could still be felt began to throb. It started to
bleed again and the pain was excruciating. He managed to keep
up, however, and even carried on an animated conversation
with Brother Richard in German. Smirnoff mused on the irony
that while Germans, Dutch and English were killing each other
in Europe, on the far side of the world German missionaries
were saving their lives. It only served to show the folly of war.

Having seen two expeditions fail due to lack of water,
Smirnoff expressed concern that there might not be enough for
the trip. Clinch smiled. 'Don't worry; it's all around you, three
or four feet down. Of course, you need a spade to dig for it,
and you need to know where to dig.'

Joe Bernard pointed to the pandanus clumps as they moved through the thick bush. 'Wherever there is pandanus there is water,' he explained, digging about a metre down. The men marvelled at the fresh water that seeped into the hole. From a shady broad-leafed tree he picked a soft yellowy-green fruit he called 'gubinge' and handed it to the men to try. It was surprisingly sweet.

It took almost three hours to travel five kilometres as the two men wounded by bullets limped slowly and awkwardly through tall spear grass. Eventually they complained they couldn't go on, so Smirnoff staggered up to Clinch and asked, 'Just how far are we going?'

Clinch hesitated, then looked Smirnoff squarely in the eye. 'About twenty miles. I know if I had told you this earlier some of you would never have attempted it. But the only way out from where you were is on foot. I had to get you going. A mile or so at a time you could attempt; the whole journey would have disheartened you.'

Despite his pain, Smirnoff agreed with the soundness of Clinch's psychology, but the men were little more than crawling by the time they reached Albert's mule team. With great relief, Smirnoff and Vanderburg were helped up into the spring cart. Brother Richard climbed up to take the reins and Hoffman was squeezed in beside him. The cart was too small to carry all of them and Gerrits and Clinch would have to walk.

It was hard to see where the narrow track they were following led, but somehow the cart managed to navigate through the sand, bush, potholes, termite mounds and mud to the mustering camp, the occupants feeling each bump reverberate through their aching bodies. At the mustering camp they were reunited with Dick Brinkman and van Romondt. They ate lightly and rested, at last well away from the nightmare of the site of their ordeal and the odour of the dead.

It was 9 March and, typically, the day was hot. They decided to rest in the shade, building up their energy with more food and sweet tea. Any more exposure to sunlight was dangerous, particularly for Brinkman and van Romondt, so they delayed travel on to the mission until the afternoon.

Word of the survivors had travelled to Broome and well-wishers had driven to the Beagle Bay Mission. From there they had begun to follow the route of the mule carts, hoping to meet up with the survivors and join in the rescue. However, since the track was not suitable for vehicles many had become hopelessly bogged and the progress of the rescuers was slowed by having to free stranded vehicles. Then, close to the mission, the mule carts suffered the same fate. A utility which they had freed moments earlier came to their rescue and the survivors and the rescue team were transferred to the back of the vehicle. Together, they drove up the dusty potholed road to the mission in the early afternoon. Horses and mules grazed inside wood and wire fences and cattle roamed around the collection of stone buildings and ramshackle shacks. Aboriginal children ran alongside the ute, smiling and waving.

Passing a green field of turf, Smirnoff remarked, 'What a wonderful spot for an aerodrome. Why don't you use it as a landing field?' Brother Richard smiled. 'Oh no, we don't want to destroy the turf, we like to look upon this wide expanse of green.'

The ute bounced along the path, passed the white church, and finally came to a standstill outside a whitewashed stone building. The men were greeted by nuns, who helped them down from the wagon and inside the dormitory which consisted of a single small room full of beds. The nuns fussed over the men, supplying them with hot water and soap to scrub off the accumulated dust, mud and blood before dressing their wounds.

The men were encouraged to rest, though beds were at a premium. Exhausted, Smirnoff lay down next to two men already sleeping there. When he woke later in the evening, he realised the two men next to him were Cramerus and Muller, whom he had last seen four days earlier. The three chatted excitedly and compared notes. When Smirnoff told the pair of the death of the little boy, Muller took the news particularly hard.

Later, in the reception room of the mission, Captain Smirnoff and the survivors joined the brothers. The captain thanked them for rescuing the group from Carnot Bay, insisting it was cause for celebration. Bishop Raible took the hint and arranged for the men to be handed a glass of red wine. Smirnoff later described it as 'the most terrific claret I had ever drunk'.

Famished, Smirnoff ate his dinner with relish, astonishing the missionaries with the amount of food he was able to put away.

During the night the mail truck arrived, and Smirnoff, Vanderburg, Hoffman and Cramerus boarded the truck for the 140-kilometre trip to Broome. The truck had no headlights and much of the journey along the corrugated track, which only the driver recognised as a road, was at night. Then a tyre blew and they had no spare, but despite this, the truck hobbled into Broome at around 2 a.m. The following morning the rest of the survivors were taken to Broome. There were plenty of vacant beds at the hospital as the injured from the Broome air raid had all been moved south. An RAAF officer provided first aid to the emaciated survivors. He told them of the air raid on Broome a week earlier and that most of the population of the town had fled in panic. Under the circumstances, nobody in Broome had given a second thought to Smirnoff's DC-3.

Smirnoff had just settled in for the night when the air raid siren wailed. Smirnoff leapt out of bed and hung over the verandah, yelling to a young policeman who was pedalling furiously towards the harbour. The policeman slowed down and pointed. 'Look there.' Smirnoff looked towards the harbour and saw four fast torpedo boats with no flags flying. As the boats pulled round the quay, Smirnoff smiled with relief as the red, white and blue flag of the Netherlands unfurled from the masthead. The craft had escaped from Surabaya and run the gauntlet of Japanese sea and air power to reach the Australian coast.

In the morning an Australian National Airways representative made a DC-2 available for Smirnoff and the other survivors to fly to Port Hedland, where better medical help was available. A handful of curious locals waved them off. At Port Hedland, the orderlies cleaned their wounds and replaced their bandages. Already it seemed to Smirnoff as though their ordeal had been just a bad dream. The bullets in his arms and hip were the only tangible reminders of the horror of the week before.

Of course, the captain hoped that one other tangible reminder would be unearthed. It would be the task of Warrant Officer Gus Clinch to return to that lonely shore to bury the dead and search for the valuable package. Before Smirnoff had left Beagle Bay, he had explained to Clinch that he felt responsible for the package as he had been entrusted to guard it. Clinch assured Smirnoff he would do all he could to find it. Neither man could have guessed that, in the coming days, the survivors would come under the scrutiny of Dutch and Australian authorities seeking to find the diamonds. Even Brother Richard would become a suspect as the mystery of the Dakota's missing diamonds deepened.

Chapter Seven

WHERE ARE THE DIAMONDS?

Diamonds were of prime importance for both the Allies and the Axis powers during the Second World War. Necessary to manufacture the millions of precision parts required for mass-producing airplane engines, torpedoes, tanks, artillery and the other weapons of war, diamonds were also needed to draw the fine wire needed for radars, for the jewelled bearings in stabilisers, gyroscopes and guidance systems for submarines and planes, and for the abrasives necessary to rapidly convert civilian industries into a war machine. The supply of diamonds was vital to keep the war machine moving.

While the demand for industrial diamonds skyrocketed, so too did the demand for gem-quality diamonds that had been stockpiled before the war. Small, durable, portable and exchangeable across borders, diamonds were used to purchase arms and finance the war machine. They offered a means to ensure that wealth survived even when countries did not. Tight controls were placed on the diamond trade for the duration of the war.

Amsterdam and Antwerp were the centre of the world trade in diamonds prior to the outbreak of war, as this was where thousands of mainly Jewish craftsmen turned the rough diamonds from African mines into finely crafted gemstones. At war's outbreak, there were an estimated 3000 Jewish diamond businessmen and craftsmen in Amsterdam. When Germany swept across Europe and looked set to invade England, the world's stockpile of diamonds was poised to fall into the hands of the Nazis.

Many diamond traders managed to escape to England and the United States, taking their diamonds with them. In an agreement with the British government, an organisation known as the Correspondence Office for the Diamond Industry was set up to register the diamonds and keep them secure for the duration of the war.

In 1939, diamond traders Willy Olberg and David Davidson joined the flow of jewellers fleeing Amsterdam, taking their families and their diamonds with them.

David Davidson had already brought diamonds, watches and jewellery to the East Indies in 1914, creating N.V. de Concurrent, one of the finest jewellers' shops in the chic upmarket town of Bandung. Situated on a plateau in the Parahayangan mountains, Bandung's pleasant climate and lush surroundings had offered an escape from the blistering heat of the lowlands since the mid-nineteenth century, when it was the heart of the region's most prosperous plantation area. Surrounded by active volcanoes, dramatic mountain landscapes, forests, cool streams and green valleys, it was to Bandung that the Dutch went to play. Hotels, cafés and shops had sprung up to serve the planters and tourists, and Bandung became known as the Paris of Java. Offering the latest of European wares, N.V. de Concurrent's clientele included sultans, politicians and businessmen.

Davidson was later joined by his brother-in-law Willy Olberg. The business flourished in the wealthy colony and in 1930 the pair moved back to Europe, where they could readily purchase the latest goods, including Swiss watches, gold, silverware and gemstones, to stock their boutique Indies business. Their jewellery workshop in Amsterdam hired only the best craftsmen, producing high-quality pieces. Willy's son, Frans, who had been brought up in the trade, had developed a reputation for precise appraisals through his careful analysis of diamonds. He had a keen eye and was able to spot the tiniest imperfection. This enabled him to select only the finest of diamonds to be fashioned in their workshop.

When they left war-torn Europe in 1939, the Davidson and Olberg families took as many diamonds as they were able to get their hands on in case the war should hamper supplies to the East Indies. But the East Indies offered only a temporary respite from aggressors, as soon war was being waged across the Pacific. Ensuring East Indies wealth was kept out of the hands of the invading enemy was the role of the Netherlands East Indies Exchange Institute (NEI). When Java looked certain to fall, the Exchange Institute negotiated the storage of valuables and money with the Commonwealth Bank of Australia. The Australian government had set up a safe repository for gold and other valuables in late January 1942 at the jail in Broken Hill, a remote mining town 1160 kilometres west of Sydney in the outback of New South Wales. Short-term prisoners had been given early release, and long-term inmates were sent to Bathurst, another rural town, so that construction on the special steel-lined concrete vault with a grille and double combination-locked doors could be built in a space between blocks of cells. In February 1942 a heavily guarded train filled with gold ingots made the transfer from Sydney to the Broken Hill jail. From the air the enemy would never know that the jail held such valuable items. Gold and coins from the Javasche Bank were transported to the hidden repository with the help of the Exchange Institute.

Word of the rescue of the survivors of Smirnoff's DC-3 filtered across mainly Dutch networks. The wounded from the Carnot Bay crash had been transported to Perth's Hollywood Hospital, still suffering from dehydration, burns, shrapnel or bullets embedded in their bodies, but for a time it seemed as if the world had forgotten them. No authorities visited or bothered to find out their story. It seemed to Captain Smirnoff that their harrowing ordeal was of no interest to anyone.

Smirnoff had been told to stay in hospital but the indignant Russian did not take well to such orders. He was desperate to get to Sydney to see Margot. He asked to see the Dutch Consul and demanded a flight east. On 15 March, after much begging and pleading, Smirnoff was heading for Melbourne.

Word travelled fast. Soon after he landed in Melbourne, the captain was approached by a well-dressed gentleman who announced himself as a director of the Commonwealth Bank of Australia.

'Is there something you want to hand over to me?' he asked with some urgency.

'To hand over to you?' Smirnoff replied, puzzled.

'The packet which you were given in Bandung.' The agitated banker's face reddened as he spoke. 'Where is the packet?'

Slowly it dawned on Smirnoff. Was he to be reprimanded over the packet after all they had gone through? 'I don't know,' he replied tersely.

'You don't know, as in it's been handed over to someone else, or—?'

'I lost it,' Smirnoff interrupted.

The banker was clearly annoyed. 'But you were entrusted to take good care of it.'

Smirnoff thought of all the things he had had to 'take good care of' in that fateful week, and somehow the package didn't seem too high on the list. Smirnoff did not want to share the details of all that he had endured, but he told the banker that the package had been lost in the sea near the plane, that he had searched the plane and the water nearby but he had not been able to locate it. 'We were more interested in water than the package,' he explained. Smirnoff asked the banker what was in the packet.

'Diamonds! Thousands and thousands of top-quality diamonds.'

Smirnoff was taken aback. He hoped the banker would understand the circumstances in which they were lost. Somehow he thought not.

The KLM director and his wife took Margot to Sydney airport to meet Ivan. She was not able to speak; tears choked her as she collapsed into his arms. Smirnoff later chastised the director for not providing him with transport to Sydney, pointing out he had been forced to beg for passage. He demanded the rest of the survivors be flown to Sydney immediately.

Finally alone together, Margot tended her husband's injuries, pleading with him to go to hospital, but he had had enough of hospitals and wanted to be with his wife. Months of fear, tension and anguish flooded out in waves of relief, joy and laughter, with the two lovers together again like newlyweds.

That night, the same people who had attended the two-minute silence in Smirnoff's memory joined him in a celebratory dinner at the Australia Hotel. Hundreds of Dutch exiles gathered in the lavish ballroom to honour the man who had managed to land an unarmed plane on the remote north coast of Australia under heavy enemy fire. But it would not turn out to be Smirnoff's red-letter day.

Also waiting for Smirnoff at the hotel were a Mr Richardson from Australian Military Intelligence and Mr van Oosten of the Netherlands Exchange Institute. On his arrival, Smirnoff was whisked away for questioning in another room. The investigators grilled him for what seemed like hours, focused on the task of getting to the bottom of where the diamonds were and whether someone had taken them. Smirnoff told the two men every detail: of the man at the door of the aircraft in Java as they were ready for take-off, the Zeroes' attack on the plane, the injuries, the dead, and the search along the shore for the valuable package.

The investigators finally allowed Smirnoff to return to the dinner, but just as he was about to eat he was called out again. Smirnoff spoke English but was more comfortable speaking in Dutch, so van Oosten often translated Richardson's questions and Smirnoff's answers.

'You say van Romondt dropped the package in the water?' van Oosten continued.

'Well, I didn't see him drop it,' Smirnoff replied.

'But he told you that he dropped it?'

'Yes, I think so.'

'And you believed him?' Richardson interjected.

'I don't know him well, but I have no reason to doubt him.'

'You are certain he was not carrying the package when he left the plane?'

'Well, no.' Smirnoff could see the look on Richardson's face, as if he thought he had it all figured out. Their questions annoyed the Russian intensely.

'Van Romondt immediately brought you your satchel, but nothing else?'

'Yes,' Smirnoff replied angrily.

'He prioritised the satchel over the valuable package?'

'I don't think it was a matter of priority. And if you are inferring that he handed the package over to me and that I played some part in its disappearance, then as far as I am concerned you will not get an ounce more cooperation from me!'

'I'm suggesting nothing of the sort,' Richardson tried to reassure him, hoping to calm Smirnoff down. It didn't work. Smirnoff was infuriated by the repeated inferences that he or one of the passengers had stolen the package. Over and over he recounted the terrifying events of that week, while the investigators honed in on each passenger's actions, looking for anything that was suspicious.

'Van Romondt—what was he wearing when he went inside the plane?' Richardson pressed.

'Actually, it was really hot, but he wore a waterproof leather jacket. I thought that was a bit odd. I didn't say it at the time.'

'Would it be possible to conceal a package in this jacket?'

'I suppose so.' Now Smirnoff was beginning to have doubts about the man.

'What about the other men? Who else entered the plane?'

'Leon Vanderburg went in when the plane was still burning,' Smirnoff answered.

'Before or after van Romondt?'

'I don't know. What difference does it make?'

The investigators didn't answer. 'Anyone else?'

'Heinrick Gerrits grabbed a few things early on, and they both returned later looking for supplies—but then again, van Romondt, Muller and Hoffman also went through the plane to collect pieces of equipment. I remember Vanderburg went through the dead woman's bag,' Smirnoff said in Dutch. Van Oosten explained the revelation to Richardson, who looked horrified.

'No one found any trace of the packet,' Smirnoff added.

'And did these men take anything with them when they left the crash site?'

'Gerrits and Vanderburg each carried a small case back to the mission.'

'What about the rescue party? Did they go near the plane?'

'Not that I saw,' Smirnoff answered. 'They were Germans, though. Vanderburg spoke German with the brother—Richard, I think his name was. They were talking the whole way back. The rest of us couldn't tell what they were saying. Those brothers at Beagle Bay were interned, but they let them out.'

Van Oosten translated and Richardson shook his head. 'The country's under attack and they let the Germans out up north. You've got to wonder, don't you...'

They didn't want to know what it was like to listen to the screams of the injured in the plane, knowing that every life was in your hands, nor what it was like to watch a man dying a slow, agonising death on the beach, nor how frustrating it was, not to be able to use your arms to hold the child who had just lost his mother. Smirnoff loathed them for their incessant questions and for all the doubts they placed in his mind. Later that night, he found himself going over the events on the beach, questioning the actions of every man.

'Why so much fuss over a few stones when nobody seemed to make a fuss about the dead—my comrades . . . the woman . . . the little baby?' he later wondered. It was supposed to be a night of accolades, instead it was a night of accusations. The guest of honour would miss most of his own party.

As the next step of the investigation, Military Intelligence worked at tracking down pilots Leon Vanderburg and Heinrick Gerrits. On 17 March, urgent telegrams seeking their whereabouts were transmitted across the country. Vanderburg was in an air force ward at Heidelberg Hospital in Melbourne, where he was, in the end, to spend six months before being discharged with a bullet still in his semi-paralysed leg. When Military Intelligence officers arrived in the crowded ward, they demanded to inspect his few remaining belongings. He willingly complied and they found nothing. Vanderburg was very sick, suffering from his leg wound, loss of blood, dehydration and burns. Doctors advised he was not up to questioning for more than five minutes. Captain Proctor of Military Intelligence in Melbourne conducted the interview. He asked Vanderburg if he had seen the package. The invalid replied that the only time he had seen it was when it was handed to Smirnoff in Java.

'Did you know what was in the package?' Proctor asked.

'No,' he replied, 'but Captain Smirnoff told me it was of very great value.'

'No doubt that intrigued you?'

'Of course,' Vanderburg replied.

'Tempted you, even?' the investigator pressed.

'It would be tempting to any man,' Vanderburg retorted. Proctor then asked what happened to the package at Carnot Bay and Vanderburg repeated the story of van Romondt losing it in the water.

'Did you go through the luggage of the dead passengers?' Proctor accused.

Vanderburg was horrified at the inference. 'I did, sir. We needed bandages, nappies, water, food. Also, I wanted to identify the dead and obtain mementos for their relatives. This is why I went through the luggage.'

'What is your relationship with Richard Bessenfelder?'

'Who?' Vanderburg asked.

'Brother Richard Bessenfelder of Beagle Bay.'

'The man who rescued us?'

'Yes.'

'He was a nice man. He rescued us.' Proctor paused, clearly wanting more information. 'We talked about living in that godforsaken place. He told me he didn't mind it, that he felt he was doing good things for the Aborigines. I told him about Java and the war. That kind of stuff.'

'You speak German?'

'Yes, I do.'

'Did you give him anything in return for rescuing you?'

'No, I did not. And I'm sure he'd be horrified at what you're suggesting.'

'The diamonds could not have disappeared. Either one of the people on that plane or a member of the rescue party must have taken them.'

'Well, it wasn't me,' Vanderburg said, his mind running through the passengers and crew of the Dakota, trying to work out who it might be.

The investigators were no closer to finding the whereabouts of the package. Proctor reported to Richardson, 'Although the interview was not held under the best of conditions, I am firmly of the opinion that Vanderburg spoke the truth. He is a young boy with no trace of guile or deceitfulness, and is believed to have been perfectly frank.'

Intelligence Officers in Adelaide interrogated Gerrits, who also said that van Romondt had attempted to retrieve the valuable package but lost it in the water. When questioned, van Romondt verified the story.

In light of the information, Major Martin wired Intelligence in Sydney on 18 March and advised them to begin diving operations at the site of the crashed Dakota at Carnot Bay as early as possible. It was also recommended that if van Romondt admitted to dropping the parcel, then, providing he was fit to travel, 'he be flown back to Broome to indicate the precise point where he threw the package overboard'.

Smirnoff still had doubts about his passengers. He contacted van Oosten on 23 March, suggesting Gerrits and Vanderburg had been put on guard by the army's direct approach. Van Oosten made note of Smirnoff's concerns: 'as they were very closely associated during the journey from the wreck, he [Smirnoff] does not attach very much importance to the similarity of their stories.'

To the Dutch owners of the diamonds, the Olberg and Davidson families of N.V. de Concurrent, the gems hardly seemed to matter. Fires blazed across Java as oil refineries and the port burned. The local radio station broadcast its last bulletin, signing off 'Until better times'. Japanese soldiers wearing caps cycled into the streets as the locals tried to come to terms with the end of Dutch rule. Families were evicted from their homes, all banks and European schools were closed, and the entire male Dutch population was interned. Ironically, it was Japanese Samurai mercenaries who had first helped seal Dutch control over the nutmeg trade and the Spice Islands of Indonesia almost 300 years earlier.

Frans Olberg broke his back defending an airstrip during the Japanese invasion. The Japanese took over the hospital where Frans lay with his back braced and turned it into a POW camp. His father Willy set up an underground movement smuggling food to the prisoners until he was captured and interned. His business was taken over by the Japanese, who kept some family members on to run the company. The town and businesses were looted by invading soldiers. Hiding under her bed, Davidson's wife gave birth to her fourth child on the day she was captured; the family was later imprisoned at Ambarawa, a women's prison camp where fights regularly broke out over the meagre rations of food, and Japanese soldiers sought 'comfort' women. Olberg's seventeen-year-old daughter Elly was interned with the Davidsons at Ambarawa.

As the families endured starvation, malaria, forced labour and beatings at the Japanese POW camps, the diamonds were the last things on their minds.

Part Two

DIAMONDS
GALORE

Chapter Eight

THE OLD PEARLER

James 'Skipper' Mulgrue, a lean old man with grey hair, a well-trimmed moustache and withered but refined features, had been sweeping the verandah at Dysons store opposite the Continental Hotel when he heard the sound of gun fire over the bay at Broome on that fateful day of the Japanese raid. Known to the locals as Skipper, from the days when he headed his own pearling fleet, the 66-year-old had watched as a flying boat erupted into a ball of flames and had heard the distant sound of screaming. Leaving the door of the store open, he had raced down to the foreshore where other locals gathered, watching as the Japanese wove in and out, picking off each aircraft one by one. When the planes had finished on the bay they headed towards the town.

Mulgrue had ducked into a slit trench near the hotel but the planes had flown on towards the airstrip and continued firing. When the danger had passed he went back to the foreshore and helped an exhausted Dutchman who had swum the long distance from the flying boat to shore. The Dutchman had pulled off his clothes to help make the distance, so Mulgrue took him up to the store and provided him with a drink and a change of clothes. Then Mulgrue drove up the long jetty, where dazed and injured half-dressed men, women and children stood shocked and confused, unsure what to do next. Even though the Dutch had been his enemy back when he had fought in the Boer War in Africa, as a soldier he had admired their fighting spirit—and these people were young enough to know nothing of that war.

Modern warfare was very different from the man-on-man battles Skipper Mulgrue had known during service in both the South African Boer War and the First World War. Somehow, it seemed a fairer fight back then. The Japanese air raid was a blip, a passing moment of unmatched strength, but the war machines of the Second World War meant the airmen could not know that their legitimate military targets were laden with civilians. They had not fired a single bullet on the town's people. Such were the great technological advances of the time that you did not look your enemy in the eye to know whether they were soldier or child.

Mulgrue guided a woman and child to the front seat of his car then returned to the jetty, directing three more men into his vehicle. When it was full, he took them first to get a drink and clothes and then to the hospital and airport. If they did speak English, they seemed in no mood to talk, so he too remained silent.

Planes arrived and went, emptying the town of its people. Anyone who had not managed to get on a plane by 2 p.m. on the day of the raid was advised to find their own way out. Nine American soldiers joined a civilian convoy of five trucks containing thirty men heading south to Port Hedland. When the road ran out, they pushed the truck through sand and detoured around the saltwater marshes, eager to put distance between themselves and Broome. Others headed south on the lugger *Nicol Bay*.

While the Japanese had not wiped out the town, in the days that followed Broome seemed to die anyway. The fear that Japanese soldiers might soon occupy the town had emptied it and robbed it of its soul. The dusty pindan streets lay deserted. Before joining the exodus, Police Inspector Jim Cowie wrote an urgent letter to the Commissioner of Police on 5 March expressing the desperation he felt in the days following the air raid.

There was a good deal of panic in the town and people immediately commenced to get away fearing an afternoon raid. The bank officials were among the first to clear out as also Mr. Cowan, Clerk of Courts and Mr. Ferguson, Fisheries Inspector. Mr. Lawson, Customs Officer also went to bush some miles out and quite large numbers of Broome people. Mr. Lawson has since returned.

That night it was announced that the Americans in town would be all evacuated by planes, which were then arriving from South, and Colonel Leggo [sic], in charge of the American forces advised everybody to get out of town by morning, as he believed the Japs would be back to bomb it. This caused a general exodus and that night after the injured people were taken away by plane, Dr. Jolly who is also Resident Magistrate packed up and left the town taking all the Hospital staff and Quarantine Officer with him. They are said to be proceeding overland to Perth by car and no intention of returning, therefore the place is left without a Doctor or Hospital facilities...

Storekeepers have all closed up and most of them cleaned out with what they could take with them by car.

Really the position is acute, as all essential services are at a standstill. No Banks are in operation, and, as far as I can ascertain the Bank Officers have taken all the money with them and do not intend to come back. We will be unable to pay Police Salaries here tomorrow.

The Hotel keepers are also talking of closing down and getting away as there is now no defence for the place at all.

Large numbers of American planes came here last night and, during the night evacuated all their men, and the members of the R.A.A.F. also have disappeared. They seem to have taken all machine guns and defence weapons with them, and the place is really defenceless, as most members of the Home Guard have also cleared out.

The Police are doing what they can and are arranging to get an old Motor truck and car in reasonable running order to take all out if finally we must go. However they will hold on to the last.

The whole town, or what is left of the people, are in a more or less state of fear and expect bombing raid or landing of Parachute Troops at any time. Particularly do they fear the possibility of landing as owing to the position of Broome, in relation to the sea there is but one road out, and that, runs along the full East side of the Aerodrome and troops suddenly landed there would trap town people from getting out.

The most despicable feature at this time is the fact of the Doctor rushing away just at a time when he may be required, and it would seem that his doing so had considerable influence on others clearing away.

In conclusion I can only say that the Officials and others now left in Broome are living in a sort of helpless anticipation of future happenings now that all form of Defence is gone.

Streeter & Male and Dysons stores reopened a few days later; the owners had stayed in town fearing looting of their stocks. But the ships that once replenished them stayed away.

Fears of invasion were not baseless, as some of those who sat in the comfort of the suburban cities of the south of Australia would later suggest. As so many cities across the South Pacific already knew, an air raid often preceded invasion. If the Japanese took Broome, then Port Hedland, Perth and Albany, the west coast of Australia would be Japanese.

Skipper Mulgrue had no desire to leave. He wondered if he had been numbed by his war experience or was just too old to bother. Where would he go anyway? His family were spread out across the world. One son, George, was missing in Europe. Another son, John, was fighting in Tobruk and a third, Patrick, had managed to get into the merchant navy despite being only seventeen years old. They had followed in the family footsteps—at least the last three generations of Mulgrues had been fighting men.

Just as his father had before him, James Mulgrue had joined the Royal Warwickshires, a British Army regiment, fighting in the Boer War in South Africa and later in the First World War in India. Returning to England at the end of the Boer War, he had met his wife Lilian. The couple eloped, marrying in a registry office, but he was restless and they set sail for Western Australia. Soon after they arrived, they set up a store and post office amidst a scattering of wheat and sheep farms near a railway siding at Isseka, which also supplied wood to the nearest major town centre at Geraldton. It was hard, backbreaking work in the Australian bush.

Taking his wife with him, Mulgrue rejoined his former regiment in India to fight in the First World War, and then in the Third Afghan War. Returning to Australia, in 1921 he moved his family north to the port of Broome after hearing from friends of the fabulous wealth being made in the pearling trade. The period before the First World War was Broome's golden age. Labour was cheap and the price of pearl shell high. The master pearlers had made huge profits and more than 400 pearling boats sailed the northern waters in search of pearl shell.

The Mulgrues had lived the high life in India during the wars, and the notion of a life at sea combined with the image of the master pearlers in white suits and topees in their verandah bungalows was very alluring.

The pearl shell had been the economic backbone of Broome since the 1860s, when seafarers noticed the beautiful pearl-shell ornaments dangling from the human-hair belts of the Aborigines. At first they had sought to trade them, until they found a plentiful supply of their own by wading out into the sea at low tide. By the 1900s Broome was supplying more than 75 per cent of the world's mother-of-pearl, the pearlescent coating of the oyster shell used in buttons. More and more men were attracted to the north-west, etching out a prosperous living on the remote coastline.

As coastal supplies were depleted, hundreds more came to scour the depths and risk their lives in hope of finding their fortunes. The white pearlers used Aborigines, Manilamen, Chinamen, Malays, Javanese and Koepangers to plough the depths for the prized shell, and Broome evolved as a town like no other, a melting pot of cultures and anathema to those who had legislated at Federation for a white Australia.

It was a business based on hard work and luck, with the prospect of riches uncertain. The indentured workers would return to their provinces wealthy men in their own right, but the wealth came at a cost—the death rate among divers was said to be as high as 20 per cent a year. The cemeteries were full of men who had died in the dangerous and laborious search for pearls and pearl shell in the shark-infested waters off Broome.

When Dutch authorities in Batavia, alarmed at the number of deaths among Koepangers and Malays, cut the flow of labour from the East Indies, the pearlers paid blackbirders to fill the labour void. On dawn raids, armed with whips, guns and shackles, blackbirders would round up healthy young Aborigines, enslaving them to work on cattle stations or pearling boats, and beating into submission anyone who protested. The captive men, women and children were forced to take on the dangerous task of diving and shelling. Those who clung to the side of the ships for too long had their fingers hit with an oar to set them off again. Challenging authority would be met with whips and chains. The use of women and children as divers was banned after a complaint from the Catholic Bishop of Perth, Matthew Gibney (who later took Ned Kelly's confession and performed the last rites), which resulted in the passing of the *Pearl Shell Fishery Regulation Act* of 1875. It was Bishop Gibney's concern for the safety of Aboriginal people that lead him to invite the Trappists to set up a mission at Beagle Bay.

Captain Ivan Smirnoff and his wife Margot returning from their honeymoon in 1925.

The pilot of the Dakota, Captain Ivan 'Turc' Smirnoff.

Daan Hendriksz
Mervyn Prime

Some of the passengers
and crew of the
Diamond Dakota.

Jo Muller in 1972
Haagse Courant

Pieter Cramerus
Pieter Cramerus

Passengers and crew of a visiting Dornier DO24 aircraft being ferried to shore in Broome, Western Australia.

Australian War Memorial neg. no. 044613

A pall of smoke rises from the burning hull of one of the six large aircraft destroyed on the aerodrome in the Japanese air raid on Broome. The plane is probably a Liberator.

Australian War Memorial neg. no. P02039.003

N.V. de Concurrent in 2005:
the diamonds were sent from
N.V. de Concurrent in
Bandung, Java, to Australia
when the Japanese invaded.
Stephen Fleay

Survivors of the Broome air raid
in 2002. L-R: Andy Ireland,
Frits van Hulsen, Albert van
Vliet, Henk Hasselo, Gus
Winckel and Harry Simpson.
Mervyn Prime

Brother Richard Bessenfelder of Beagle Bay with a cup given to him by Ivan Smirnoff.

The West Australian

Joe Bernard, a member of the rescue team.

The West Australian

James Mulgrue, one of the three men charged with stealing the diamonds. The photo was taken in 1919 when he was a captain in the British Army serving in India.

Major Clifford Gibson. Gibson enlisted Palmer, who spilled thousands of diamonds across his desk in Broome.

Mervyn Prime

Jack with his blue Chevrolet, 'Bluebird', which he bought after the war.

Courtesy of Broome Historical Society

Jack Palmer unloading oil onto a lugger.

Courtesy Battye Library ref. no. 010848d

The Australian Army team at Carnot Bay in front of the crashed Dakota in 1942. Jack Palmer is third from the left wearing a singlet. Lieutenant Laurie O'Neil is second from the left.

Courtesy of Broome Historical Society

The *Aumeric* at low tide in 1943 after the army requisitioned it from Mulgrue and Robinson. It was later destroyed.

Australian War Memorial neg. no. 051734

Connie and Willy Chatwell in 1968.

The West Australian

A cross at Carnot Bay commemorates the four people who lost their lives in the crash.

Daniel Balint

The remains of the Dakota in the water at Carnot Bay in 2005.

Daniel Balint

As the shallower pearling fields were depleted, the Aborigines refused to don the claustrophobic vulcanised canvas suits, massive bronze helmets and lead-weighted boots required for deep-sea diving and were largely replaced by Japanese divers after the turn of the century. The Japanese divers would spend hours underwater, often almost horizontal as they peered into murky waters through inch-thick face plates, frantically placing oysters and pearl shell into their collecting bags.

While the master pearlers made their bread and butter from pearl shell, they always dreamt of finding that pearl of pearls. Such was the allure of the pearl that men risked their lives in the hope of finding them, and a bustling trade in 'snide' or stolen pearls emerged in the frontier town.

When the Mulgrues arrived in Broome in 1921, the town was a straggling mile of wood and corrugated-iron shops, with sharp racial and social divisions among the inhabitants. The pearling crews worked hard and played hard. Chinatown's Sheba Lane offered a bustling array of favourite pastimes, including drinking, fighting, gambling and prostitution. Even with endless acres to build on, the Asians preferred crowded quarters with their own kind to the stand-offish reticence of the scattered bungalows of the European master pearlers.

Money was good in the early days, and Mulgrue and his family enjoyed the life of master pearlers, living in a wood and iron bungalow on stilts, surrounded by a broad latticed verandah and shaded by flame-red poinciana trees, frangipanis and palms. The roads that linked the bungalows of the master pearlers, maintained by gangs of Aboriginal convicts, shimmered white from the grit of pearl shells. Malay and Aboriginal servants tended to their needs, ensuring 'Captain Mulgrue' had clean and pressed white safari suits. Lilian ordered her dresses from London and busied herself at the local church.

The heady profits of the early days were already gone when Jim Mulgrue got in on the action, but there was still money to be made. For three years he enjoyed the good life, but by the mid-twenties the signs of the impending Depression were already visible, and the market for pearl shell began to bottom. While the Depression did not hit as hard in Broome as in some parts of Australia, most of the lugger masters could not afford the fuel for the air compressors for the divers, and reverted to hand-turned pumps. The bungalows of the master pearlers were left empty and the Asiatic quarter began to fall down.

James Mulgrue and his crew were still pulling in pearl shell, but London was not paying a good price for it. Mulgrue struggled to put food on the table—meals were often bread and dripping— and he lost two of his luggers to his creditors. Added to this, he began consorting with other women and Lilian left him.

Jim Mulgrue managed to hold on to the lugger *Dragon*, but the shell price never recovered despite new and rich pearling fields being discovered. The *Dragon* was at sea when a devastating cyclone decimated the pearling fleet in 1935. One hundred and forty-two men died, and twenty of the thirty-six luggers based in Broome were lost. The *Dragon* and Skipper Mulgrue survived, but the vessel was extensively damaged. The *Dragon* was repaired and Skipper continued pearling, but the market did not improve—more than a hundred Japanese vessels began working the northern waters, flooding the market and driving the price of pearl shell down further. Mulgrue joined the clamour of European pearlers demanding action, and in 1935 the Commonwealth agreed to help subsidise the industry. As the market tumbled, some lugger captains sold their boats to the Japanese illegally, a process called dummying. In 1938, James Mulgrue retired from pearling, aged sixty-two. Pearling had failed to fund his retirement, and to fill in the extra hours he took up work at Dysons store and sold chickens to the local butcher. With a regular salary, he was not quite so subject to the vagaries of the economy, the wind and the weather.

Broome was his home, where as a former master pearler he still commanded some respect, where the old-timers could talk of the hardships, snide pearls and vast profits of the old days, and where the locals all knew him by name.

The Continental Hotel was normally one of the liveliest spots in town, where men from the sea drank, gambled, shouted and sang, spinning yarns about their adventures, dirty deals, murder, ghosts, cyclones, dangerous sea creatures, lost sons, the old days when the money was really good and, of course, the pearl of pearls. Here Mulgrue spun rich stories, engaging people with the crinkle of his eye and his smooth educated accent. Here, too, with the flicker of an eye or the lift of a finger, men with an illicit pearl tucked in their matchboxes gave the signal to a snide buyer willing to give hundreds in cash for a pearl worth thousands in London or Paris. But the mood in the bar after the air raid was sombre and melancholy.

'Bloody Japs!' Mulgrue quipped to a soldier at the bar. 'Not content to take all our pearl shell, now they want the bloody country!'

'You were in the pearl industry?' the soldier asked, and Skipper nodded. 'Ever find a big one?' the soldier continued.

'I've found a few,' Skipper replied, 'but it isn't pearls that have kept this town going. Shirt buttons that won't crumble in the wash have brought more money to Broome than all the pearls in the Sultan of Baroda's famous pearl shawl.' He remembered the tales of the phenomenal treasures held by the Indian Sultan from his time in India. The Gaekwar of Baroda was reputed to own a pearl rug that was three metres long and almost two metres wide, with some diamonds woven in for good measure. 'Pearl shell, not pearls, keeps the industry going and always has done.'

Crippled Canadian motor mechanic Frank 'Robbie' Robinson sat on a bar stool sipping on his beer, which he held with a twisted arthritic hand, listening to the conversation. Robinson had owned a motor garage in Broome for the last eighteen months, but the military had taken it over in the weeks leading up to the air raid. He too had helped the survivors to the hospital and the airport after the attack. Born in Canada, he was not the type to settle in one place. He was another drifter, having worked in ports around Australia and the world, and Broome was full of drifters. He had set up his business after leaving Cockatoo Island—an iron ore mine off the coast north of Broome, where he had worked for BHP as a diesel electric engineer—when arthritis had got the better of him. Now his leg was so twisted and gnarled he could barely walk.

'What are you going to do now?' the soldier asked Mulgrue.

'Couldn't stand going down south,' Mulgrue replied. 'All that cold weather and the people, they're different in the cities.'

Robinson chipped in, 'Colonel Legg reckons everyone should get out. Says the Japs could land any day.'

The soldier nodded. 'I don't have any choice, I go where I'm sent, but if I were you, I wouldn't be sticking around.'

'Where would I go?' Mulgrue replied.

'I've got a chance to take Mr Kennedy's lugger away from Broome for him,' Robbie told Mulgrue. 'I could do with an experienced sailor like you.' Bert Kennedy, known around Broome as 'H.K. Unsinkable', owned seven luggers, a schooner, a store and the state shipping agency. He feared his fleet might be decimated in another Japanese attack and wanted to get the boats out. Robbie was one of the few left in town who knew anything about sailing. It often amazed people how a man as disabled as Robbie could work his way around a boat, but he couldn't sail it alone.

'He isn't interested in where we go but would like me to take it south, somewhere out of harm's way,' Robbie continued. He looked at the Englishman, who appeared old and tired and didn't seem much interested in going anywhere. He was a decent bloke, Skipper, and even in his sixties he was still able to pull the ladies in. If he had to hang out on a boat for a few months, Skipper was one of the few blokes he wouldn't mind spending time with, and he'd heard the older man had been a good captain in his day. 'Personally, I don't want to go south—it's too cold for my crippled leg and arthritic hands—but Kennedy said south,' Robbie explained, adding, 'It's the *Aumeric* and it's motorised.'

'I'm not going south,' Mulgrue told Robbie.

Robbie was eager to get out of town and needed Skipper's boating skills. 'We can take it north. North's good,' he explained.

Mulgrue told him he was prepared to stay in Broome and face the consequences, but he'd think about his offer.

Over the next few days, the town became increasingly deserted, and the handful of residents who remained were anxious. Stocks were low, communications were down and there wasn't even a doctor in town. Everyone feared the Japanese were about to land.

Mulgrue made up his mind to accept Robbie's offer to take the *Aumeric* north, providing they could sort out money for stores and agree on a destination.

Robbie was pleased that such an experienced boathand as Skipper Mulgrue would accompany him on his way north. They discussed locations along the coast that would provide fresh water and good campgrounds for sitting out the war. They agreed on Cape Leveque, as the lighthouse keeper had a pedal radio which would enable them to get news of the war. The more they talked, the more excited they became about the idea.

Mulgrue collected the wages owed to him by Dysons to fund supplies and petrol for the trip. Now that he had made up his mind to go, he was relieved they would soon be on their way. After stocking up with eight months' worth of stores and selling off the goats and chickens, they were ready to set sail when the tide allowed.

Two weeks after the air raid, on 18 March, the crippled mechanic and the pensioner sailed on the midday tide on the B45 lugger *Aumeric* with two Aboriginal crewmen. The Dampier Peninsula was lined with creeks and little bays ideal for hiding a lugger. Heading north as they had planned, they were armed with three rifles and a machine gun in case of trouble. The weather was hot and still, with ominous storm clouds looming overhead. As the tides receded, rocks and reefs raised their ugly and potentially devastating heads. It was the tides that determined every move of the sailor and his craft, and many a boat had come to grief on the shoreline for failing to respect the tides. They left on the neap tide, but poor winds made the going slow.

They sailed past the wreckage of Smirnoff's Dakota at Carnot Bay, the site of so much tragedy, but did not go near it. A week after the raid, news of the rescue of survivors from the Dakota had spread through the town like wildfire. Robbie had travelled with a friend to greet them but had been bogged. Mulgrue had stayed in town as he had to mind the store. When they brought the first lot in, Mulgrue had sold a singlet that was miles too big to a young, skinny pilot with an injured leg. The pilot had given him Dutch East Indies currency, which wasn't much good, but it was more than the survivors from the raid in Broome had been able to offer.

The coastline near the crash site was exposed and the waters filled with sharks. The tide was going out and they did not want to get stuck at Carnot Bay, where there was no ready supply of fresh water near the shore. The devastation in Broome was still fresh in their minds as they travelled north. Their intention was to get as far away as possible from the war and all its casualties, and the bullet-ridden Dakota was a reminder of the time in which they lived.

The lugger passed a stark red bluff that protruded from the coast; at the base, the vivid rouge sand from the bluff cut a line across the white sand which led down to the sea. A billowing cumulus cloud crept across the sun, throwing out beams of light at odd angles. Moving northwards past rolling dunes, they rounded Sandy Point, entering the broad expanse of Beagle Bay in the afternoon as the sky blackened and winds whipped up the ocean. The *Aumeric* heeled and rolled through the rising stormcaps which threatened to swamp the boat. The mainsail and mizzen were lowered for fear of damage. They headed towards Normans Creek, where the sand had been whipped up into a frenzy. The wind eased, lightning cracked and thunder roared above, and then driving rain fell. Drenched through, they sought shelter below deck.

Normans Creek provided refuge from the storm. When the rain subsided they decided to move on into the Beagle Bay settlement to access the freshwater wells there.

Warrant Officer Gus Clinch had returned to the crash site at Carnot Bay with Brother Richard five days after they rescued the survivors of the crash. On arrival, he had reburied the bodies of Daan Hendriksz, Joop Blaauw, Maria van Tuyn and Jo van Tuyn. He had searched the interior of the plane for the missing package, but found nothing.

On 29 March he received orders from his superior, Major Gibson, to return to Carnot Bay and retrieve a radio set and to again search for the package. He heard Mulgrue and Robinson had moored their pearling lugger at the creek and headed down, hoping to hitch a ride south.

Jim Mulgrue's eyes were bandaged but he heard Clinch approach.

'Who's that?' he shouted.

'It's just me, Gus,' Clinch replied. Robinson turned and waved, and Clinch sat down to join them.

'You blokes are lucky you got out of Broome when you did.'

'What's happened now?' Robinson replied, alarmed.

'The Japs have been back. Bombed the town this time,' Clinch advised.

A 'V' formation of seven Japanese bombers had flown over Broome on 20 March, releasing about forty bombs. They targeted runways, wireless equipment, petrol dumps and other buildings at the aerodrome but luckily most of the bombs missed their targets. The raid claimed one life, that of a Malay, Abdul Hame Bin Juden.

'Anyone left in town?'

'A handful of soldiers, a couple of old-timers,' Clinch explained.

Mulgrue lifted his bandage, revealing red, watery and swollen eyes, but he couldn't bear the sunlight and covered them again.

'What's up with your eyes?' Clinch asked.

'Sandy blight,' Mulgrue explained. 'Caught it in a sandstorm.' (Sandy blight is, in fact, trachoma, a chronic bacterial eye infection which can lead to blindness.)

'Which way are you blokes heading?' Clinch inquired.

'We thought we'd hang out here for a bit, then maybe go up to Cape Leveque,' Robinson replied.

'Did you pass the Dutch plane?' Clinch asked.

'The DC-3?' Robinson asked, and Clinch nodded. 'Is that the plane the Japs shot down a couple of weeks ago?' Robinson wanted to know.

'I helped rescue those blokes. They were a real mess. Could barely walk,' Clinch said.

'They brought those blokes back to Broome but I didn't see them. You did, though, didn't you Jim?'

Mulgrue was not in the mood for conversation. His eyes were driving him mad. 'I served one of them at the store,' he said abruptly.

But Robinson was glad for the company and asked Clinch to recount the tale of the rescue of the Dutchmen.

The soldier obliged, finishing by saying: 'I have orders from Major Gibson to go back out to the plane. I was hoping I could hitch a ride on your lugger?'

Robinson looked to Mulgrue, who squinted beneath the bandage. 'Even if I could bloody see, the tides aren't right. The boat's neaped [run aground on the very low tide] and we're not expecting another good tide for days.'

'Between you and me, and it's not to go any further, it's not just a radio set I have to search for,' Clinch explained, hoping to sway the old man. 'That plane had a fortune in diamonds on board and I've been asked to fetch them.'

Robinson's eyes lit up, but Mulgrue calmly repeated, 'Can't help you. The boat's neaped and I can't see.'

Clinch wasn't sure whether it was the boat that wouldn't budge or Jim Mulgrue but he had to take his word for it. The major had asked him to report back in a week, so he rounded up a group from Beagle Bay and set out to Carnot Bay on foot.

While he knew the way, the trip was still long, hot and unpleasant. This time, Clinch found a piece of string with two wax seals, a piece of white wrapping paper containing half an imprint of the seal of N.V. de Concurrent, and another piece of white paper with the word 'Comm'. It was the first evidence of the package's existence retrieved from the site, but there was still no sign of the contents of that package.

Jim Mulgrue and Frank Robinson stayed in Beagle Bay for about ten days, fishing and mixing with the Aborigines and generally whiling away the time. Mulgrue's eyes improved, but water supplies at Beagle Bay were low and the pair thought it best to move on.

When the next spring tide rolled in, Robinson and Mulgrue hauled anchor and, using the tides to carry them northwards, headed for the bountiful fresh water supplies and good camping grounds of Pender Bay. Along the coast, red pindan cliffs jutted into the Indian Ocean, interspersed with barriers of mangroves, white sandy beaches and grey gums. The land was neither jungle nor rainforest nor desert. It is a place that looks like no other, ancient and worn.

A small crescent bay known as Middle Lagoon lay just south of Pender Bay, and the men decided to moor the lugger here. It was one of the prettiest bays on the peninsula, with crystal clear water and a broad white sandy beach. A red and black rocky headland at the north side of the bay curved around, giving protection from the westerly wind. The pristine sand was smooth and untouched except by the multitude of beautiful coloured shells, corals and sponges at the tide line.

They anchored the lugger and rowed to shore. Robinson and Mulgrue set up camp in an old wooden pearler's shack that lay in the protection of the dunes surrounding the beach. It was badly damaged and offered little protection from the weather, but at least there was a freshwater well and native blackberry trees provided both food and shade. After setting up camp, they walked over to the headland which harboured food for the picking. Climbing through large rock walls whose natural arches provided windows to the sea, they picked up rocks covered in oysters and took them back to their camp. They chipped the oysters from the rock, prised them open, and ate the succulent meat inside.

Shells washed up on the beach, including huge trumpet and trochus shells, and they too were full of food. Robinson and Mulgrue had been there about four or five days when the lugger *Eurus* sailed into the bay, mooring right alongside their boat. On board was larrikin beachcomber Jack Palmer.

Chapter Nine

THE BEACHCOMBER

While elsewhere in the world man tamed and stripped the land to use for his own purpose, it was apparent to even the earliest explorers that on the north-west coast of Australia nature's forces would mock any efforts to tame them. Cyclones sank pearling fleets and razed whole towns, and birds and plagues of insects devoured crops. Tides surged forward like floods, causing rivers to rip through island passages, curling down around headlands and cascading off reefs. Small boats had been known to disappear completely in the convulsing waters. On the low tide, an inviting sandy shore could be transformed into a derelict mudflat only a crab could enjoy. Months of dry weather, cracked mud and salt plains would be followed by torrential wet season downpours, blackening the sky and filling rivers and lakes that spilt across the plains and crashed down over ridges. Along the coastline, the rivers' prodigious wet season floodwaters collided with the sway of the tides.

Bold dreams to build cities and populate the land would never eventuate. Settlers often found the steamy hot days, powerful weather and nights filled with the drumming of insects too oppressive, and departed for gentler climates. The northern coastline is littered with stone remnants of would-be towns, a few crumbling headstones the only reminder of the people who came with dreams of a new life only to have them shattered.

Some managed to etch out a living on the remote coast, more often than not lured by pearls or gold, while others came to escape their past and hide in a place that was seemingly a world away from it all, drifters who found the pace of the modern world did not suit them. These hermits and beach-combers sought to find a lonely shore where one could carve out a niche and enjoy the fruits of nature in splendid isolation.

Jack Palmer was such a man—his tanned leathery skin told of years in the sun, and hidden beneath his bushy moustache was the laconic smile of someone who enjoyed life. He was a drifter, an uneducated man, who liked the company of people too much to be a hermit. If Jack had a colourful past he didn't share it. He was thirty-six when he arrived on the north-west coast from New South Wales. No one knew what he was escaping from or what led him to eke out a life on the lonely bays, for the Kimberley was one of those places where people didn't ask too many questions about your past.

For ten years Jack had lived the life of a beachcomber, shunning the demands and obligations that were part of normal urban living. He preferred to live in the open, exploring the absolute freedom of uninhabited islands and untrodden shores, discovering the moods and inclinations of bays and coves, jungle-covered hilltops, reefs, bluffs and precipices. The war only served to further convince him that living away from it all was the only way to go.

One of Jack's favourite pastimes was hunting for dugong—the large slow-moving sea cow resembling a seal with a large head and a huge, pendulous, rubber-like underlip studded with sharp bristles. The flesh of the young dugong was highly prized by the Aborigines, and Jack enjoyed the sweet and tender meat which was not unlike beef, and the dry-cured blubber that tasted like bacon. He also knew how much the fare impressed his Aboriginal women friends, of whom he had many. Relationships with Aborigines were frowned upon by Broome's segregated European community but, as a beachcomber, Jack was far away from their watchful eyes.

There were two types of beachcombers who lived in the tropics of Australia. There were naturalists like Edmund Banfield, who wrote of the free and easy life of a beachcomber on Dunk Island in northern Queensland in 1908, recording in minute detail the wildlife, flora, people, geography and moods of his isolated world. His ramblings about a deserted tropical island, where he swam, fished and hunted at leisure, inspired many dreamers to follow his course.

And then there was the type of beachcomber that Banfield abhorred. This type of beachcomber chose to live alone to carry out his selfish deeds away from any scrutiny. It was not unknown for such a beachcomber to hasten the demise of a ship to secure its bounty. These men were known to bully Aborigines out of their copra, coconut oil and pearl shell. Living from what they could get from the sea or from the Aborigines—turtles, turtle eggs and fish—they sometimes overpowered the local Aborigines and took their women.

Jack Palmer had not been known to hasten the demise of any ships, but many considered him lucky not to have been on the receiving end of a spear or club. But then again, luck was something Jack possessed in full measure.

Jack had twice run foul of the law for taking Aboriginal women of mixed descent on board his boat. Pearlers, sailors and farmers were banned from taking Aboriginal women and children of mixed descent without permission from the Protector of Aborigines, but there were few authorities patrolling the coast. Where there was law enforcement, it nearly always went in favour of the white man.

Jack Palmer had heard of the air raid on Broome from the lighthouse keeper at Cape Leveque and was heading back to Broome to stock up on supplies. The lighthouse keeper had been told to keep his light off in case of another attack and been given a radio so he could maintain contact with the military authorities in Broome. As he no longer needed to tend the light, he was given the role of looking out for Japanese aircraft and reporting any unusual activity on the remote coast via coded radio messages. More than a week had passed since the air raid when Jack passed through on his gaff-rigged lugger, the *Eurus*.

During the Depression, men who'd sought their fortunes in pearling in better times gambled away their luggers just to get out of Broome. Jack had never said how he came by the *Eurus*, but it was never registered in his name. The old lugger was a shadow of her former self. In the heyday of pearling, before the First World War, the *Eurus* played an integral part in Broome history. At sea, the tall-masted pearling lugger cut a romantic figure along the barren and isolated shores of the north-west coast. It was on board the *Eurus* that a bold experiment to replace indentured Asian labour with white divers first went horribly wrong in 1912. The Federal Government didn't like the large number of Asians making a fruitful living from pearling on the remote western coastline and took action to replace them with white divers. But most of the pearling masters were opposed to this new policy—while Asian labour was paid at £2 per month plus a commission for shell raised starting at £15 a tonne, the British divers were to be paid £13 per week with £40 a tonne commission. So when English deep-sea divers donned the heavy metal diving helmet and cumbersome canvas suit and descended to the depths, most of the European masters and the local Asian population hoped they would fail.

In this environment, English diver William Webber set sail on board the *Eurus* for Ninety Mile Beach, as Broome was then known. For two weeks he descended daily from the decks of the lugger into the clear waters, scouring the sea floor in a heavy diving suit for hours, searching for the prized shell. He was disappointed by the amount of shell he found and feared the repercussions of failure. At a later Royal Commission into the pearling industry, other divers claimed they were taken to fields that were known to be poor.

In June 1912 Webber's body was taken from the *Eurus*. He was the first of the white divers to die from the bends— a crippling paralysis that claimed the lives of many divers in the harsh north-west. Subsequently, two more of the twelve English divers died and all contracted the bends, some several times. Before the season was out, all had withdrawn from the pearling fleet. The local Asian divers and their employers were jubilant.

By the time the Second World War arrived the *Eurus*, built for hardiness rather than grace, had seen better days. With peeling paint, the ingrained odour of shellfish, worn timber decks, a patched-up hull and infested with cockroaches and rats, the old lugger was picked up by Jack Palmer.

Palmer reached the shores of Roebuck Bay some time around the second week of March. March was the lay-up season, a time of year when storms and the threat of cyclones meant the luggers were pulled up on the beach and the crews either travelled home or stayed in town, visiting the pubs, the gaming houses and brothels of Chinatown.

Normally dozens of pearling luggers lined the beach, generally in trenches, so they could be reconditioned ready for next season. But when Jack sailed in, the luggers had all moved elsewhere. Broome seemed like a ghost town. Jack walked down Sheba Lane, a place normally brimming with life. It was here that a Japanese man had tattooed the rising sun on Jack's left arm. Today it was completely deserted, the bordellos, gambling dens, shops and bars all shuttered.

On the way down to Broome from Cape Leveque, Palmer had seen the wrecked plane on the beach at Carnot Bay and decided to report the sighting to Broome police. Sergeant Jim Cowie told Palmer that the passengers from the DC-3 had been rescued. He asked Jack if he had boarded the plane, and Palmer assured the police officer he had not.

After reporting the wreck, Palmer headed down to Dysons to stock up on supplies, fearing the store might be closed or that his credit had again run out. He was relieved to find it open, although stocks were low. He took what he could—flour, tea, sugar and tinned food, the main staples—and loaded them on his boat.

He hung around town for a few days, but talk of imminent invasion was rife, so he decided it was best to move on. Calling in at the native camp he asked an Aboriginal couple, Bonnie Bundigora and Tinker, if they would like to get out of Broome and sail north as crew on the *Eurus*. Tobacco and food were all they could expect for their labour. They agreed—the police had already advised them to leave as no Aborigines were allowed in town. They rigged the *Eurus* and waited for the turn of the tide.

Jack Palmer, like all seasoned Kimberley sailors, timed his journey to work with the tide, which could outrun a boat travelling at ten knots. Sailing out of Roebuck Bay with the tide, the *Eurus* headed north, passing an arena of reefs, russet-toned outcrops with an ancient, time-worn presence and white sandy beaches, waters that Jack knew like the back of his hand.

Late in the afternoon, Jack ordered his crew to prepare to tack towards Carnot Bay. They looked at each other nervously; the bay was about ten kilometres across and dry most of the year except when the king tides filled it. As one of the least attractive and treacherous bays on the coast, it was a place that most chose to avoid. They sailed past Cape Baskerville at the mouth of Carnot Bay, dodging the reef, towards Red Bluff. They spotted the Dakota on an exposed part of the shore, but dangerous reefs, rocks and the tides prevented them from mooring too close. Jack generally preferred to stay away from anything to do with the war—or so he later claimed—but the chance of finding good salvage was too good to resist.

He had made extraordinarily good time from Broome to Carnot Bay and arrived just before the sunset. The tides and winds were in his favour. Anchoring the lugger, he ordered Tinker to ready the tender and then he climbed on board. The oars dipped into the black and silver water as the sun sank below the horizon; above, an orange sliver of light melted into green and then a vast purple sky. The black outline of the plane sat abandoned on the beach. The crash survivors had been rescued only days before. Tinker hauled the tender up onto the soft sand. Jack had to walk some distance to reach the bullet-ridden Dakota. He pushed open the door and hoisted himself up into the blackened cabin, where he began to pore over every crack and crevice of the aircraft, on the lookout for anything worth taking.

It was relatively dry inside the burnt-out interior. A blackened suitcase had managed to survive the fire and Jack was able to retrieve some clothing which he tossed out to Bonnie and Tinker. They were delighted with the find; the war had caused a desperate shortage of clothes. Jack found a beautifully decorated Javanese basket and took that for himself.

The wind roared in through the broken glass of the cockpit and the orange light was fading fast. As he moved towards the cabin, where the light was best, he saw the bullet holes in the seat where Maria van Tuyn had sat with her baby, and where the bullets had pierced the seat of Captain Smirnoff. The sea had washed the blood away. Palmer was amazed that anyone could have survived such an onslaught. Looking inside the captain's safe, he found it empty.

Jack's hands gently felt from side to side, sifting through the sand that had filled the bottom of the craft. He dug down into a crevice between the supporting ribs of the petrol tank near the pilot's seat and felt a damp paper package wedged in there. Lifting it out, he looked at the address: 'Commonwealth Bank, Sydney'. The package was tied with string and had two red wax seals across the seams; one was a crown, the other a bank seal.

He considered taking it back to Broome and forwarding it to its planned destination. But then again, it had been left out in the middle of nowhere, so maybe it wasn't anything particularly special. Opening the parcel was like opening an oyster shell. He had pulled open many, hoping to find one magnificent pearl that would change his fortune. He'd found a few decent ones, even one lying loose on the beach, but not enough to make a difference. The wax seals came away with the string as he pulled on it. He ripped off the soggy white wrapping paper. Inside was a straw box about the size of a cigar box, which he tore apart to reveal a bloated leather wallet. He was relying on touch now. There was no light left in the aircraft, just the dull grey of night, which could be seen beyond the broken windows. He opened the wallet. There were a number of compartments inside bursting with tiny tissued packages. He pulled one out and unwrapped the tissue paper, feeling the tiny hard stones inside. His hands were calloused from pulling ropes, and it was too hard to separate one out to hold up to the dying light. He wished he'd brought the lantern from the boat. In his heart, he felt they were gems, but he tried to refrain from getting excited until he could examine them more closely.

He climbed out of the Dakota and called to the crew, 'We're going back to the boat!'

'There's no moon tonight, boss!' Tinker said. 'Can't see the boat, or the crocodiles.'

'Get in the bloody boat!'

The three of them rowed in the black of night to where they thought the lugger was anchored, but it was so dark they couldn't find it. Jack was agitated, desperate to verify his hopes of finding a treasure. After rowing around in circles for a while they gave up and returned to the beach, where they slept on the sand not far from the graves dug only days before, where two men, a woman and a small child lay buried.

The next morning, in the light of day, they made their way back to the *Eurus*. Jack kept the wallet concealed from the two Aborigines in case they got any ideas. He climbed below deck and put the ornate Javanese basket on a shelf in the cabin. He yelled to Bonnie and Tinker to lift anchor and sail north for Beagle Bay. Then, sitting down, he opened the brown leather wallet. He again pulled out a small package wrapped in pale blue tissue paper and carefully unfolded it. Inside were hundreds of glistening, finely cut diamonds. He opened another packet and then another, pouring out the contents and watching them clatter onto an enamel plate. He gazed, spellbound, as the lights of a king's ransom blazed back at him. Thousands and thousands of diamonds lay before his eyes. It was a salvage like no other he had ever known.

'I'll be buggered!' he exclaimed, gathering up handfuls of the stones and holding them up to the light of the morning sun streaming through the hatch. At first he had wondered if they were real, but as he watched the many facets of the jewels glisten in the sunlight he had no doubt. Some were as big as shirt buttons. 'I'll never have to work again,' he said out loud. Poking his head out the cabin door he yelled to Bonnie and Tinker, 'I'll never have to work again!' He grinned jubilantly and went back to admiring his booty.

Chapter Ten

THE TREASURE

Beneath the billowing canvas sails of the old lugger, Jack Palmer's tobacco-stained fingers gripped the wheel of his craft. A broad grin was hidden by his bushy moustache as the wind carried Jack and his treasure northwards.

Beagle Bay was only a short trip by lugger from Carnot Bay. Palmer sailed into the bay and up the creek, anchoring not far from the mission. He let off Bonnie and Tinker and took on two other Aboriginal crewmen, Stephen and Peter. He had no intention of stopping, and moved out quickly before the tide subsided to leave him high and dry in the mud. Jack Palmer sailed north towards the lighthouse at Cape Leveque. The lugger sat flat in the mostly calm waters; the only sounds were the waves lapping against the hull, the ropes flapping against the sails, and the creaking of the wooden mast, the calm lull occasionally broken by a sharp order from Palmer to his crew.

At the entrance to Hunter Creek, just south of Cape Leveque on the tip of the Dampier Peninsula, he passed two pelicans who appeared to be standing guard. Curlews and other marsh birds waded along long white sandbars. Ibises called out as they flocked from the dark green mangroves whose aerial roots provided a haven for a nursery of marine animals. The fishing was good at Hunter Creek. As the tide receded a feast of fish, including trevally, Queenies, barramundi and mangrove jacks, became trapped in the holes and were easy fare.

Jack spotted Christy Hunter poking a sharp stick down a crab hole in the mangroves. Hunter was a Broome resident whom Jack knew well. A crab clung to the stick and Hunter pulled it off—careful where he put his hands, as the crab's huge claws could easily break a finger—and threw it into a bucket.

Jack rolled up his trousers and waded on to the sandbar. Hunter, who'd come off a lugger moored further upstream, came over to trade a mud crab for tobacco. 'Come over to the lugger later on and I'll get you some,' Jack said.

On the beach, Jack Palmer boiled up a pot of water and threw in the mud crab, watching until it turned orange. Pulling it out, he waited for it to cool, then ripped off the huge claws and smashed them open with a rock, extracting the succulent white meat inside.

Later in the day Hunter came to the *Eurus* for the promised tobacco. When Palmer went into the cabin to get it, Hunter looked in and noticed the ornate bamboo basket that Palmer had retrieved from the crashed Dakota. Palmer explained he had found it on the wrecked plane at Carnot Bay.

Hunter had helped transport some of the survivors from the plane when the spring cart had become bogged on its way to the mission at Beagle Bay. He remembered their distress vividly. 'Those men were in a bad way,' he told Palmer. 'Barely said a word the whole trip—a couple of them had bullet wounds, too. They reckon the Japs kept strafing them, even after they'd crashed.'

'Apparently four or five of 'em died,' Palmer added.

'Brother Richard told me there was a woman and baby on board that didn't make it,' Hunter said.

'Poor buggers!' Palmer said, shaking his head. During the conversation Hunter continued to stare at the unusual basket. Palmer took it off the shelf and handed it to him, and Hunter admired the intricate design. If Hunter was impressed with the basket, Palmer couldn't wait to see his reaction to the other surprise he had found in the wreck of the plane. Opening up his suitcase, the beachcomber took out the leather wallet and opened it. He removed one of the blue tissue paper parcels and, cupping it in his hand so as not to spill the contents, carefully unwrapped it, revealing the diamonds. Reaching into the pile he took out a diamond the size of a button and placed it in Hunter's hand for him to admire. 'I don't have to work now, I'll just sit down and smoke,' he bragged. Hunter had never before seen anything like the beautiful gemstone he held in his hand. But after a few seconds Jack snatched it back, placing it inside the tissue paper, and returned it to the wallet.

Later in the day, Hunter told Jack he'd come across some Dutchmen who had fled Timor on a boat. 'These blokes are in a really bad way. You should see the state of their lugger.'

'All the way from Timor, you reckon?'

'Apparently they started on a power boat but it ran out of fuel. They found this wreck of a boat on an island and managed to make it here.'

'Shit, eh! It's a bloody long way,' Jack replied.

'Lucky to be alive,' Hunter said. 'Ginger and I are going to sail with 'em up to Cape Leveque. Check their boat doesn't sink. They can get water and make radio contact with Broome from there. Better get going. We're heading off as soon as we're rigged.'

'I'm heading up there tonight. Maybe I'll see you there,' Jack said.

The lighthouse at Cape Leveque stood like a sentry, tall and white atop huge sand dunes, guarding the entrance to King Sound and warning ships of the dangerous rocks and reefs nearby. The lighthouse keeper's cottage was a regular meeting place for the pearlers and fishermen who sailed the Dampier Peninsula. Nearby was the Catholic mission of Lombadina, which was, like the Beagle Bay Mission, run by the Pallotine

Brothers and the Sisters of St John of God. Another Aboriginal community lay a short distance away at One Arm Point.

Pirate, navigator and explorer William Dampier had landed in the area near Cape Leveque more than 250 years earlier, in 1688. William Dampier and Palmer shared many traits. Like Dampier, Jack Palmer possessed the same indomitable spirit that led him to search for adventure beyond the familiar world. He was a rebellious character, who loved the freedom of life at sea away from the watchful eyes of authority. Both the buccaneer who stepped ashore so long ago and the beachcomber Palmer had long dreamt of finding great treasures.

Dampier spent the summer months of 1688 around Cape Leveque and King Sound, but he was not keen to stay, despite wanting to find a place to escape the clutches of the crew whom he feared would kill him. (He later published a damning report on his visit to the Australian mainland.) Dampier was destined for greater things, circumnavigating the globe three times and later recording his voyages and mapping part of the Western Australian coast and New Guinea.

Dampier was not the first Englishman to land on Australian soil. Sixty-six years before, in 1622, the *Tryall* was wrecked on the reefs of the Monte Bello Islands off the north-west coast. The captain and forty-five crew made it north to Batavia in two longboats, leaving ninety-five men behind to perish. Since the *Tryall* more than a thousand ships have come to grief on

Western Australia's 10,000-kilometre long coastline. Some contained treasures—silver coins and gold sovereigns or legendary pearls. The cursed Roseate Pearl is said to lie at the bottom of the sea on board the ill-fated steamship *Koombana*, which sank in a cyclone in 1912.

Hunter and Palmer caught up with each other again at Cape Leveque.

'So they made it around without sinking,' Palmer remarked, pointing up the creek to where the Dutchmen's lugger was moored.

Hunter nodded. 'They don't speak any English, so it's a bit hard to work out what's going on. It's a bit like charades trying to communicate with 'em.'

'Too hard, I reckon,' Palmer quipped.

'About the diamonds . . .' Hunter had done a lot of thinking about the diamonds and become increasingly concerned about the repercussions if Jack kept them. 'The men from the crashed plane at Carnot Bay are alive. They probably passed on a list of what was on the plane to Gus Clinch. And if they have, the army will be out looking for them and they'll find out the diamonds are gone. You gotta hand 'em in.'

Palmer looked dismayed. It was a fair find, but if the military were out looking, trading the diamonds might be difficult. The thought of discovering so much wealth and treasure only to hand it in was too much to bear, but then again he wasn't sure he had much choice. 'Give 'em to Gus,' Hunter urged. 'The army will know what to do with 'em.' In the end, Palmer agreed with Hunter and sailed out the following day for Beagle Bay.

Palmer clutched the wallet closely as he disembarked and headed towards the white spire of the church at Beagle Bay. He was told that Clinch was off on army business and would be away for days. Ironically, Clinch was at that time looking for the very diamonds Jack had brought to the mission.

The place was teeming with people and resources were clearly stretched. Saying nothing about the diamonds to anyone, Palmer headed back to the *Eurus*, hauled anchor and headed north again. Just before Pender Bay, he sighted James Mulgrue and Frank Robinson's *Aumeric* anchored on the western side of Middle Lagoon. Palmer, despite knowing any number of points where he could anchor, selfishly moored right in front of the *Aumeric*. Before heading to shore he looked for a container to conceal some of the gems. Removing the broad round bases from a pair of chunky blue plastic salt and pepper containers, he emptied the contents and placed the diamonds inside. Lighting a lantern, he held the leather wallet over the flame, watching as it blackened, sending acrid smoke into the air. The wallet was too distinctive. He then hid the salt and pepper containers among his belongings on the boat.

He climbed down the rope ladder and waded through the shallow water, walking across the beach and over the dunes looking for the owners of the *Aumeric*. Mulgrue and Robbie were sitting down to a billy of tea at the old pearler's shack when they heard a voice over the sand hills calling, 'Are there any white men here?' Robbie stood up and waved. Palmer ran over gleefully, shouting, 'It's great to meet up with a couple of white bastards!' Mulgrue was taken aback by the enthusiastic greeting. He had seen Palmer at the store, but did not know him personally. Jack was the type of person he normally tried to steer clear of—the kind who meant trouble.

Robbie made Palmer a cup of tea, which he slurped enthusiastically from beneath his walrus moustache, pausing only to ask if they had a rifle they might sell. Robbie and Skipper had a machine gun, three rifles and a double-barrelled shotgun but not much ammunition. They offered Jack a rifle, which he took gladly. These days everyone wanted to be armed in case the Japanese arrived—besides, a gun was always handy to protect against a hungry crocodile, or to hunt bush turkey or dugong.

It was late afternoon, and by the time Jack had set up camp about fifteen metres from Mulgrue and Robbie, the sun was setting. Robbie had caught a good-sized barramundi and invited Palmer to join them for dinner. Mulgrue had the feeling that Jack was in the habit of skiving off others, but it wasn't his fish so he didn't protest.

That night Mulgrue went to bed early and Jack stayed up talking with Robbie by the firelight, trading stories they'd heard about Broome and the war. They were bitter about the minimal military support that had been sent to defend their region.

'The bastards down south have deserted us,' Palmer said.

'Bloody idiots have no idea,' Robbie added, drawing back on his cigarette. 'I could imagine the bloody fuss if it was Sydney or Melbourne that was attacked. Then they'd bring every bastard back from helping the bloody Pommies.'

'That's for sure,' Jack agreed.

'They sent Major Gibson, but he's only got a dozen or so soldiers. Fuckin' may as well give the bloody place to the Japs for all we matter.'

'Tried to join up a couple of months back,' Palmer said. 'Got knocked back because of me ulcer.'

'I didn't know belching and farting was a good reason to knock you back!' Robinson laughed.

'You wouldn't be laughing if you had a bloody ulcer.' Palmer looked hurt.

'I was only joking. I reckon they'd take you now. Spoke to Gibson before I left. He's bloody desperate, mate! He even asked me and I can barely walk.' Robbie was rifling through his bag as he spoke, searching for aspirin to ease the pain of his arthritis.

'Is that right, eh?' Jack replied. 'I might just do that. Reckon I'd like to give those Japs a whipping.'

Robbie found the aspirin bottle and swallowed a couple of tablets. He shifted from his seat and lay down in the sand where it was more comfortable. 'What about those poor buggers at Carnot Bay? Did the Japs get stuck into them, or what! Poor bastards. Spoke to Gus when we stopped in at the mission a few days back. Reckons there's a packet of missing jewels out there somewhere.'

It was the opening Palmer had been waiting for. 'I found 'em,' he said.

'Bullshit!' Robbie replied, sitting up suddenly. 'We were going to take Gus out there but the tide was out. You're not bullshitting me, are ya?'

'Wait here,' Jack said, getting up and jogging back to his boat. He returned moments later. Pulling over a camp stool and placing an enamel plate on it, Jack slowly began pouring the diamonds from their unlikely plastic homes.

Robbie picked up a particularly large diamond and held it up in awe, watching the flames dance through its many facets.

Mulgrue always rose early. He had a billy of tea boiling and damper cooking by the time Jack got up, but there was no way Mulgrue would be inviting the beachcomber to share them. His infected eyes and his mood had not improved much.

Jack set about boiling his own billy and baking his own damper, and when he finished he pulled out the salt and pepper shakers and again poured the diamonds onto the enamel plate. Mulgrue walked past, lifting his bandage a little to see where to step, and Jack called him over.

'What do you think of these?' he asked.

Mulgrue squinted down from beneath his bandage, his face close to the plate. Thousands of tiny gems came into focus. He was stuck for words.

Jack enjoyed Mulgrue's reaction and tried to stifle a laugh.

'What are you going to do with them?' Mulgrue asked when he finally found his voice.

'Don't know. Maybe give them to the Dutch and collect a big reward,' Jack replied.

The old man walked away. He needed to gather his thoughts. A big thundercloud threatened overhead but it turned out to be what the local girls in Broome called a 'male storm'. It approached belching, threatening, full of bluff and wind before only spitting and then leaving grumbling.

Later that day, Palmer joined Robbie and Mulgrue at their camp, carrying the plate of diamonds, some still wrapped in tissue paper. It was hard to talk or think about anything else but the diamonds on the plate. They examined them. Some were huge. They thought about counting them but decided there were too many.

When Jack went to return them to the salt and pepper shakers he said some didn't fit. They looked at the pile of leftover diamonds on the table. Robinson later said Jack could have fitted all of the diamonds back into the containers but he was willing to play along with the game. 'You'd better take these as a souvenir of the Japanese raid. Goodness knows you'll never be able to use them if we are invaded by the Japanese,' Jack said.

All three agreed the normal salvage fee was 20 per cent, so at the very least Jack deserved a portion of the find.

Jack gave Mulgrue a heaped teaspoonful of diamonds and Robinson a few more. Sitting around idly in the shade of a native blackberry tree, smoking cigarettes and drinking sweet tea, they discussed what they would do with their share. Jack said he knew a man in Perth who would dispose of them for him.

Mulgrue asked Palmer if he could trade a few of the smaller ones for large ones to send to his family. Palmer picked out five big ones.

Gazing at the largest of his diamonds, Mulgrue said, 'I'm going to give one to my boy in the war and one to my wife. The rest I'll try and sell to a Chinaman in Broome.'

Suddenly realising that he had given Mulgrue some of the largest gems, Palmer asked for them back, offering to replace them for a spoonful of smaller ones. Mulgrue begrudgingly returned them in exchange for a greater quantity of lesser diamonds. He was annoyed, but put them in his bag anyway.

After a little more conversation, Palmer and Robinson moved away and began muttering between themselves. Mulgrue was sure they were planning something behind his back. Sandy blight still robbed the old man of vision, the discomfort adding to his sense of frustration. The damp bandage provided a little relief, but without being able to see what was going on he had a sense of being left out. He went over to the pair and asked accusingly what they were up to.

'What's it got to do with you?' Jack rebuffed. 'You never found anything!' Jack thought Mulgrue was being ungrateful. 'I thought you could spare another one for the lad,' Mulgrue asked. 'I mean these little ones won't fetch a tenth as much as the big ones.'

'If you don't want the diamonds then give them back. I need the bigger ones. I thought there were more of them,' Jack replied.

Mulgrue went to his bag and took out the diamonds. He walked back to Jack and flung them onto the enamel plate. 'They're just trouble anyway,' he said, and stalked off angrily.

'I suppose you want mine back, too?' Robinson asked. Jack reached down and picked out the larger ones, leaving the smaller ones. 'You can keep those—they're only dusters [very small diamonds],' he said.

Palmer was blasé about the diamonds and left them lying on a camp table, some falling into the sand as he moved his enamel mug or shuffled his belongings. It annoyed Mulgrue that the beachcomber could be so irresponsible with such an important find.

On the following day, Mulgrue and Jack made their peace. Mulgrue was sitting at his table when Jack walked over carrying the enamel plate. He scooped out a handful of small diamonds and put them on Mulgrue's plate. 'Present for you.'

Mulgrue looked down at the diamonds, everything still blurry. He pushed them across to Robbie. 'Pack them up for me, will you?' The Canadian said he would look after them for Mulgrue and put them with his own share.

'You won't say anything about them, will you?' Mulgrue urged. 'No one will know we have taken a few.' The other two agreed.

Mulgrue then advised Palmer to hand in the remainder of the diamonds to Major Gibson and claim a reward. But Jack had decided to travel to Perth to sell the diamonds.

The next morning Jack left on foot for Broome. The *Eurus* was still well stocked with supplies and Jack offered Robbie and Mulgrue the radio, two bags of sugar, tinned food and eighteen bags of flour for £30. The lugger was thrown in for free. The three men shook hands on the deal.

Taking his diamonds with him, Palmer headed off through the bush towards Beagle Bay. As soon as he was out of sight, Robbie sifted the sand where Jack had proudly shown off some of his booty and found twelve diamonds.

Chapter Eleven

AN ATTACK OF CONSCIENCE?

Jack Palmer combed his hair and smoothed his moustache, then wiped his grubby hands on his shorts. Sitting on the long shady verandah of the old Magistrate's Residence in Broome, he waited for Major Clifford Gibson to see him.

Palmer clutched his rucksack to his chest and smiled at the thought of the reaction he might get. He hoped the major would swallow his story. He had just found them, he reasoned—salvage, finders keepers, etc. Why, he should get a medal for handing these in now!

He wanted to join the military, to help fight the Japanese, and surely they wouldn't turn him down. Most people, including the military in Broome, were expecting an invasion.

After the second attack on Broome the military command in Perth were advised that the only option for Broome was a scorched earth policy; evacuate all locals, drove cattle south, and destroy anything that might be of value to the enemy. The aerodrome runways were mined with the object of destroying them if the Japanese looked set to land.

News of attacks on other Australian towns along the north coast added to the unease felt across the top end. Two days after the second attack on Broome, Katherine and Darwin in the Northern Territory were bombed, and the day after, 23 March, Wyndham was hit again. While Australia's southern capitals were kept in blissful ignorance of the extent of the attacks, it seemed to the residents in the north that their days were numbered.

Unconfirmed reports claimed Japanese submarines were using islands off the Kimberley coastline for resupply, and that Japanese commandos had been seen on the northern mainland. Long-range reconnaissance patrols by the 3rd Australian Guerilla Warfare Group were later sent to the north, but they found no official evidence of Japanese landings. Rumours of espionage and invasion ran rife. Some intelligence reports bordered on the hysterical (one of the nuns at Beagle Bay was accused of having a transmission set in her piano). Later, evidence would emerge revealing that the Japanese had been actively gathering intelligence in Australia in the lead-up to the Second World War and that incursions occurred along the northern coastline during the war.

The residents of Broome had good reason to be worried,

with a complete lack of military personnel and equipment making them extremely vulnerable.

So poorly resourced and understaffed was Major Gibson that he had to cadge ammunition from visiting US air crews and salvage equipment from the wrecks of Dutch planes, like the radio he had sent Clinch to get at Carnot Bay. He had just twenty troops under his command, armed only with rifles. He knew that a hundred armed Japanese soldiers could occupy Broome with its current defences. It was clear that he was to receive little support to defend the north of the state, yet that was the job he had been sent to do. Major Gibson needed any man he could get.

When Jack Palmer entered Gibson's office, it was more than a month since the Dutch plane had crashed at Carnot Bay. Palmer stood to attention and gazed at the wall behind Gibson's chair, declaring, 'I want to enlist. I've walked 105 miles, all the way from Beagle Bay, to join up.' In fact, he had hitched a ride with one of the brothers from the mission, but Jack was never one to let the facts get in the way of a good story.

Jack explained that as a beachcomber he knew the area like the back of his hand. Local knowledge was a skill much in demand—the military called on many locals in remote outposts to keep watch on the coast and report any unusual activity. The reality was that the massive uninhabited coastline was almost impossible to police.

Gibson sized up the dishevelled bronzed beachcomber with the short square jaw and bushy moustache. It made Jack feel uncomfortable—authority figures had always done that to him. 'There's something else,' he said, clumsily pulling the salt and pepper shakers from his bag. The major eyed the shakers and wondered where this was going. 'Thought you might be interested in these,' Palmer continued, fumbling with the base of one. He flicked it off onto the ground, spilling some of the contents. 'Found 'em in a paper parcel in the wreck at Carnot Bay. The wrapping broke up in the water, but I managed to recover these from the shallow water.' He poured the diamonds over the major's desk.

The major stared dumbfounded at the fortune before his eyes. Until this moment the diamonds had just been words in a telegram; to see them in the thousands, scattered across his desk, was something else. He paused for a moment. It was Gibson who had sent Clinch out to search for the lost package. He thought how strange the turn of events were for this small Australian town. In just over a month, Broome had become a virtual ghost town, complete with dozens of fresh graves, including small ones. German missionaries had arrived with a bunch of Dutch survivors who'd been marooned on a remote beach, and now this grubby larrikin walks into his office and splashes diamonds nonchalantly across his desk as if they were sweets.

He watched as a few diamonds rolled onto the floor near a large crack in the wooden floorboards, horrified that the man could be so careless with such valuable jewels. 'Is this all of the diamonds?' the major asked.

Palmer shifted uncomfortably. 'I was hunting dugong round Carnot Bay way and I thought I saw something in the water. I reached down and picked it up but the wrapping all broke up into little pieces and there was these diamonds falling. You can imagine, I couldn't believe it. I was trying to stop 'em from falling and picking 'em all up, but you know, well some were lost in the sand and the sea.'

'Would you be willing to show us where this happened?' Prior to joining the armed services, Gibson was Western Australia's chief prosecutor. He was trained to spot holes in people's stories.

'Sure. Sure. Well, I'll try, but what with the tides and everything... Well, it's pretty exposed. Have you been up that way?'

'I do not know the spot, no. You must have seen the crashed plane?'

'Yeah, but I didn't go near it. It's sort of like a war grave, isn't it? What with all those people, you know.'

'You didn't go near the plane at all?'

'Nah, nah.' Palmer shook his head as if he abhorred the idea. 'I'll show you where it is, though.'

'You weren't tempted to keep a few for yourself?'

'No, sir,' Palmer replied. 'Thought I'd do the right thing, it being a military plane and all. That's why I'm here, and because I want to help.'

Palmer was clearly proud of himself for handing in the diamonds and again asked the major if he could join up. Gibson looked down at the report on Palmer that lay before him. He had been rejected on a number of occasions due to medical problems, and while there may have been some holes in the larrikin's story, at least by enlisting the man he could keep an eye on his whereabouts.

And so Jack Palmer was appointed a coastwatcher at Gantheaume Point, looking out across the sea at the mouth of Roebuck Bay, where 120 million-year-old dinosaur footprints could be seen at low tide. The Japanese planes had flown over Gantheaume Point when attacking Broome a month before, claiming so many lives. It would be Jack's job to look out for planes, ships or any sign of enemy activity, and to inform authorities of anything suspicious. It would be a lonely job away from the close scrutiny of senior officers, the type of job that suited a beachcomber.

Jack left the major's office pleased he had the job. He was disappointed there was no mention of a reward for the diamonds he had handed in. But Robbie had insisted there would be a big reward, so Jack reassured himself that this might yet come.

Major Gibson carefully returned the diamonds to the salt and pepper containers, and immediately contacted army intelligence in Perth to find out what he should do with the enormous cache he now held in his office.

While Palmer was pouring diamonds over the major's desk, the Dutch official van Oosten had been making his way back from

Carnot Bay with Gus Clinch. It was Clinch's fourth trip to the crash site. Van Oosten had been sent north by Dutch authorities on 10 April to search for the diamonds after interrogating the survivors of the crash. A gang of labourers was organised to conduct a thorough search of the aircraft. At the wreck site the battered plane sat in the sand like the remains of a beached whale. At low tide, using ropes and muscle, the Dakota was hauled clear of the sea, water and sand pouring from bullet holes and cracks in the fuselage as it was hauled above the high tide line.

Clambering aboard, van Oosten painstakingly searched every nook and cranny, sifting through the layer of sand that covered the floor of the wreckage, reaching into sand-filled crevices beneath the floor in case the package had dropped into a cavity. His search yielded another few pieces of the tissue paper thought to have held the diamonds, and ten pieces of carton which, when put together, formed the sides of the packet that had held the wallet full of diamonds. But he found nothing more. The search was meticulous and thorough—the group scoured not only the inside of the plane but every inch of the beach for a couple of kilometres up and down the coast.

On the beach he found a few banknotes in the currency of the Netherlands East Indies but no further trace of anything to assist the investigation, and the group returned to Beagle Bay. When van Oosten heard of a very high tide that had flooded the coastline near the plane the week before, he concluded that the package had been lost to the sea.

On arriving back in Broome, he checked in with the major, asking about a rumour he had heard about a 'John Palmer of the RAAF' who was said to have visited the plane. But the major had been advised by Military Intelligence in Perth to keep word of the diamonds secret until they could be secured properly in Perth, so he advised that 'Mr Palmer of the RAAF' had not returned from Perth to Broome. Mr van Oosten left Broome on 21 April believing the diamonds were all still lost.

Three days after Palmer's visit, Gibson flew to Perth to hand the diamonds over to Colonel Mosely of Military Intelligence. Before his meeting with the colonel, he joined his wife and son for breakfast in Perth. Both were astounded when he poured a pile of diamonds onto a plate from blue salt and pepper shakers, swearing them to secrecy. Gathering them up, Gibson drove to the army barracks where Colonel Mosely took possession of the diamonds, later calling on the Perth head of the Commonwealth Bank, Alfred Ward, who had already been advised by the bank in Melbourne of the impending arrival of the package.

Broome police had notified the Criminal Investigation Branch in Perth, which instituted its own enquiries. Major Gibson confirmed to Perth police that the diamonds had been found. He recounted Palmer's story to detectives and told them that the military had the matter in hand.

Police reported to Ward at the Commonwealth Bank that they were not satisfied with Palmer's claims. Ward communicated their concerns in a letter to the Governor-General of Australia. Ward wrote, 'From reports received, the packet when picked up consisted of a leather wallet and the whole enclosed in a cardboard box and wrapped. If this be so, Palmer's alleged statement that the packet, being water soaked, broke in his hands when picked up, requires some further explanation.'

Ward explained in the letter that van Oosten had recovered pieces of the box and wrapping from inside the plane during his search with Gus Clinch. He wrote:

> The string and portion of outer wrapping, which Mr van Oosten is to produce to you, indicate that the string was pulled off without cutting and the paper wrapping torn. These facts, coupled with what the police now advise, point to the deliberate removal of the diamonds either by one of the passengers who hid the inner packet on the beach or by Palmer, who, when he learned that not only the police but Mr van Oosten were making enquiries, became alarmed and handed the diamonds to Army Headquarters with the story of having found them on the beach.

The bank arranged for the diamonds to be counted by Arthur and Charles Williams, of Dunklings (later Mazuchelli's) jewellers. They counted 4571 diamonds then valued at £18,500, some as large as shirt buttons and between three and ten carats, beautifully cut top-quality stones. It was quite a find.

Two of the diamonds weighed more than seven carats—the estimated value of these diamonds in today's terms is US$160,000 each. A five-carat flawless diamond included in the parcel has an estimated value of US$300,000 on its own.

There was scepticism about Jack's story, but no one suspected that there were many more diamonds to be found.

On 5 May, three weeks after Palmer handed in the diamonds, Major Gibson called on him to make a written statement explaining how he had found them. Palmer stuck to his original story, still claiming he had been hunting dugong half a mile north of the wrecked plane when he discovered a black object embedded in the sand and covered by water. Palmer stated:

> I stooped down to pick it up, but it fell out of my hand. The material seemed to be rotten. The object seemed to be made of leather and was black in colour.
>
> The tide was then on ebb and I waited until it had gone out before I examined this wallet or packet. At full tide this wallet or packet would be covered over by about eight or nine feet of water.

He described how he picked up the wallet which collapsed, diamonds falling into the sea. He scurried to retrieve the valuable gems, but many disappeared into the sand as he did so.

Nearly all the diamonds which had been in this packet fell on the sand at the beach where I had found it and I had to pick some of them off the sand.

I handed them to Major Gibson as I believed the wrecked plane belonged to the army, and I thought it was my duty to report and hand over the property to them. I did not go near the plane at any time.

Palmer asked about a reward. Gibson said it wasn't up to him.

Later in May, Jack Palmer was asked to return to the crash site with a search party to recover any stones that might have been overlooked when he had opened the package. Lieutenant Laurie O'Neill and Warrant Officer Clinch joined him, but as Jack scoured the site with his colleagues he knew there were no more diamonds to be found.

On 6 June the diamonds Palmer had handed to Gibson were delivered to the Commonwealth Bank in Melbourne, along with 275 boxes said to contain foreign coins. The diamonds were revalued in Melbourne at £20,000.

No one knew exactly how many diamonds were sent from Java. The documents revealed there were sixty-five lots, though the quantity in each lot was unknown. The Australian jewellers had separated them into 138 lots but it was clear that the method for separating diamonds in Australia was different from that used in the Netherlands, so a Dutch diamond merchant was called in. The diamond merchant stated that it was the practice in Java not to offer lots of less than between ten and twenty carats per lot. When he sorted the diamonds handed in by Palmer, there were only twenty-four lots, leaving forty-one lots unaccounted for.

As news of the diamond find hit the headlines, jewellers and businessmen from around the world cabled the Australian government outlining their missing packages of diamonds from Malaya and Java, and seeking assurances that their jewels were not among those found by Palmer.

Diamonds other than those sent by N.V. de Concurrent were apparently missing, as the flight of wealth joined the flight of people fleeing war-torn countries.

For example, the Netherlands Purchasing Commission in New York issued a telegram requesting confirmation of the source of the diamonds. They claimed that a shipment of diamonds sent out on 15 January from Batavia had gone missing, and suggested the beachcomber's cache could have been part of that consignment.

The Commonwealth Bank advised that the diamonds found by Jack Palmer were solely from N.V. de Concurrent.

Frank Robinson and Jim Mulgrue were still keeping clear of Broome, living off their supplies and the fruits of the sea. They had shifted camp from Pender Bay further north to Little Creek, which had good camping grounds. It was about a month since Jack Palmer had ambled into their camp with his amazing find. Robbie thought the entire episode was like something out of a book, and Mulgrue was still convinced the whole thing meant trouble. They had pooled the diamonds that Palmer had given them, and stored them in a metal film canister which Robbie kept in his shirt pocket. They had no idea what had happened to Jack Palmer since he departed with his fortune, and were startled when they saw him making his way along the beach dressed in a military uniform, his moustache well trimmed and hair neatly combed, accompanied by a military patrol. He was part of a group assigned to destroy all transport along the coastline, in case of invasion. Boats could be used by the enemy to move their troops or weapons further south.

As the patrol made its way along the beach, neither Robbie nor Mulgrue moved, waiting for the party to come to them. They did not know why Jack had sought them out, or why he had come with the military. They feared it was something to do with the diamonds.

Jack greeted them like long-lost friends, while Mulgrue acknowledged Jack apprehensively. Whispering to Robbie to say nothing about the diamonds, Jack said loudly, 'We're here about the luggers, mate. We can't leave transport lying around for the Japs to use. We have orders to destroy them.'

Robbie explained that the *Aumeric* belonged to Bert Kennedy, and the soldiers agreed it was in good enough condition to be of use to the Australian Navy. The *Eurus,* however, was barely seaworthy and would have to be destroyed.

Mulgrue screwed up his eyes, looking at the two luggers sitting on the sand, their white canvas sails gently waving in the breeze. He remembered the pride he felt when he purchased his first lugger and sailed out at the helm, with his boys waving him off on the shore, sharing his dream of finding the one pearl that would turn their lives around.

He sat in the shade on the sand some distance away to avoid the heat, and watched through blurry eyes as they poured fuel over the *Eurus*. The fire started slowly, the smoke driving cockroaches and rats from the hold as the lugger burned, then exploded. A huge bonfire soared into the sky, the glowing flames engulfing the ship and then climbing up the mast. The smell of petrol filled the air and the heat from the fire added to the oppressive swelter of the day. In minutes the *Eurus* was a charred wreck and the history in which she shared—the cyclones she had survived, the divers in their iron helmets and lead boots, shell cleaners prying open the oysters and scraping the meat away, men from all over Asia chattering over hot coffee and tobacco—went up in smoke. Of the fifty-two luggers that patrolled the coast before December 1941, only six would survive the war.

'Roll up your swags, you're coming with us,' the patrol leader said to the two men. Two of the soldiers would sail the *Aumeric* back to Broome, but Mulgrue and Robinson were to travel in the truck.

The soldiers offered to help the men pack up their camp but the pair turned them down. Robinson hoped to hide the film canister filled with his and Mulgrue's diamonds when the soldiers weren't looking. Palmer tried to distract them but the group were disquietingly close. Grabbing his shaving gear, Robinson placed the film canister which held the diamonds into his shaving basin and started heading towards the truck that would take them out of Little Bay. While Palmer was talking to the soldiers, Robinson dropped the canister and attempted to conceal it by kicking loose sand over it. He wished he had more time to hide it properly.

A group of Bardi people from Lombadina Mission came down to camp at Little Bay to fish and hunt for crabs as their people had done for centuries. Their camp was not far from Mulgrue and Robbie's. Connie Joorida watched as Mulgrue and Robinson headed off in the truck with the soldiers. Her husband, Willie Chatwell, had left with them. Like the beachcomber Palmer, she had often found useful items left behind by visiting sailors and was not one to miss an opportunity. While she was a traditional Bardi woman who lived off the bounty of the sea and the land, she enjoyed the odd European luxury, like tobacco.

When the group was out of sight she went down to scour their campground for cigarette butts. Sifting through the soft white sand, her fingers touched a solid object. She pushed the sand away to lift it up. It was a metal film canister, and when she looked inside she saw it held hundreds and hundreds of shiny glass stones. She would have preferred tobacco.

She took the tin back to her camp and left it hidden there until Willie arrived back about a week later. She wasn't sure what to do with the stones, and had a feeling that they might be bad luck. When Willie looked at the stones he didn't know what they were, but he was pretty sure he could get something for them. He knew the white fellas liked shiny things. In the old days, men had died fighting over pearls. The couple decided to head back to Lombadina Mission, where Willie offered a man called Jacky eleven of the shiny stones for a tin of tobacco. Willie was happy with the deal and Jacky was confident he could trade the pretty stones. He headed to Beagle Bay, where he met up with Sebastian De La Cruz, a Manilaman who worked in Broome. Jacky asked what he would give him for the eleven white stones, and De La Cruz gave him two tins of tobacco and four shillings. Jacky claimed he had found the stones somewhere between Wyndham and Derby. Neither knew what the stones were worth, but both suspected they were of some value.

Trading among the Aboriginal people continued, and the diamonds had passed through a number of hands by the time stories about Palmer's find surfaced. It was known that the amount of diamonds received from Palmer was not the full amount of diamonds that had been in the package handed to Smirnoff in

Java. With the army, Dutch officials and the police all searching for the diamonds, some of the Aborigines began to get nervous about the shiny glass stones. The police were beginning to ask questions and warning of trouble for anyone caught with the stones.

Iron neck shackles and chains were still in use in the Kimberley during the war, and the Aboriginal population were terrified of the police. To this day, the Aboriginal locals say that many diamonds were flung into the well and the springs near Beagle Bay as panic about the consequences of being found with them spread.

Major Gibson travelled to Beagle Bay with the officer in charge of Native Affairs, Mark Knight, hoping to find news of more diamonds and to discuss tactics for the mission should invasion occur.

Nervous about holding on to the white stones that were generating so much official interest, Willie Chatwell decided to give the diamonds that he still had to Major Gibson. He stood anxiously at the door of the reception room at Beagle Bay, signalling to Mr Knight to come outside. Willie gave him the metal film canister. Lifting the lid, Knight saw the container was about two-thirds full of diamonds. 'Connie found 'em up at Little Creek Bay. We didn't take 'em, Mr Knight. I swear. That old fella and the one with the funny leg left 'em behind.'

Knight assured Willie he was not in trouble and that he had done the right thing by handing them in. Returning to the reception room, Knight handed the canister to Gibson, who looked inside it and raised his eyebrows. The bank had insisted there had been more diamonds in the original shipment than those handed in by Palmer, and now there was proof positive.

Connie and Willie were rewarded with clothes and tobacco, with the hope this would encourage further cooperation and information from the native population.

On returning to Broome, Gibson sent an order to Palmer to return to headquarters immediately. The town was still deserted. There were no women and children, and of the resident population a mere forty-five men remained, mostly pensioners. Only ten houses were occupied by their original residents. Although some houses were used by soldiers, most had been abandoned with their furniture and furnishings intact, gathering dust and cobwebs. Lawns grew wild and then wilted in the hot sunshine. Homes and shops had been looted.

Palmer had expected to get some reward for handing in the diamonds and thought maybe that was why the major wanted to see him. But on arrival, he could tell immediately that he was in trouble from the tone of the major's voice.

'Come in, Palmer,' he shouted. Jack apprehensively entered Gibson's office and stood nervously at attention before his superior officer. 'You didn't tell me the truth, Jack.'

Jack could feel a lump form in his throat. 'What do you mean, sir?' he asked, wondering just what the major knew.

'There were more diamonds, weren't there, Jack?'

'I handed them all in. I swear, sir,' he replied.

'Then what are these?' the major demanded, showing Jack the film canister.

Jack looked down; he'd been caught out. 'They're the ones I gave you,' he lied.

'No, Jack, they're not. Do you want to tell me about Jim Mulgrue and Frank Robinson before you get yourself into any more trouble?'

Inside, Jack was furious but he was trying not to show it. He wondered what the hell the two men had told the major. Had they dobbed him in? 'I was just trying to protect them, sir. Him being an old man, and the other a cripple.'

'How about you make another statement? This time—the truth!'

Jack relented and admitted he had given some diamonds to Mulgrue and Robinson, but he still insisted that he had kept none for himself.

Gibson next sent for Frank Robinson. When confronted with the canister of diamonds, Robinson agreed Palmer had given him some. He told the major he had buried the canister on the beach at Little Creek when the patrol came to burn the luggers. 'Mulgrue got none,' he insisted.

Next it was Mulgrue's turn. 'I am not such a fool as to get mixed up in all of that,' he told the major.

Gibson told Mulgrue that he did not believe him and that he expected Mulgrue back at eight that evening with the diamonds he had received.

Mulgrue returned to the major's office that night and admitted to receiving ten or twelve diamonds and pooling them with Robinson's in the film canister. He said he held no other diamonds aside from those in the canister found on the beach by Connie Joorida.

Major Gibson later told the *Daily News* he released the two men when they said they knew of more diamonds. 'They said they would bring them back. That was my big mistake. I let them go and they didn't come back. I never saw those diamonds. I suppose some people would say I took some. I had plenty of opportunity but I had a lot of other things more important than diamonds to worry about.'

Major Gibson took the canister to Military Intelligence head-quarters in Perth on 16 July. Five days later Mark Knight, the officer in charge of Native Affairs, brought in another eighteen diamonds he had received at Beagle Bay from the Manilaman, Sebastian De La Cruz. Believing it was likely that more diamonds were held by Aborigines throughout the area, it was suggested a reward be offered to entice them to hand them over. Still no reward had been offered to Palmer.

Together with a Broome police constable and an Aboriginal tracker, Mark Knight travelled to Aboriginal communities across the Dampier Peninsula in September, six months after the Dutch plane crash. He questioned the locals and asked for any news of the missing diamonds. They found no more diamonds during the trip. On returning to Broome, Knight cleaned out the glovebox of his car and was about to toss out a dirty matchbox with the other rubbish when he noticed a tuft of cotton wool peeping out from inside. Opening the box he found another sixty-one diamonds. He knew they hadn't been there four days earlier when he left on the trip.

With evidence of more diamonds having been found, Military Intelligence and the Dutch authorities agreed the investigation should now be handled by the Western Australian police force. Detective Sergeant Albert James Blight had joined the police force when he was twenty-three years old and had been a detective for eighteen of his nineteen years on the job. The controversial cop would be dismissed from the force a decade later on charges surrounding the treatment of illicit gold tailings and withholding information in relation to jewellery thefts. Blight would work closely on the case with Inspector Cameron, who had been sent to replace Cowie after his hasty departure from Broome, and with the military who were in control of the area. With news of more diamonds appearing in the Kimberley he headed north, hoping to build a career-making case against Palmer in what was becoming a national headline story.

Blight summoned Palmer to the Broome police station, where he had set up a temporary office. He demanded the coastwatcher come clean. Palmer said he had already made two statements and had nothing further to add, but when presented with evidence of further diamonds he agreed to make a third statement to 'tell the truth and get it over'. He said he found the paper parcel containing the wallet with all the stones, which he put in a bamboo basket on his lugger, but insisted he had handed all of them in to the military aside from those given to Frank Robinson.

'I was going to keep them for a while, sell some of them to the chaps in Broome and then take the balance south and get rid of them. Later I decided to enlist and hand the diamonds over to the military authorities. Robinson told me that if I handed them over I would get a good reward.' After further questioning Palmer said, 'The military got all the diamonds I had in my possession except the few I gave to Robinson and Mulgrue. They were lucky to get what they did, for if I had known as much then as I do now the military would not have got any of them.'

Detective Blight tracked Robinson down in Derby. Blight recorded Robinson's version of events and then warned him he might face charges. Robinson told Blight he believed the diamonds were salvage as Palmer had found them, and if Palmer had not recovered them before another tide had come and gone, the diamonds would probably have vanished forever. 'There may be a court case in Broome, and before you sign this statement I tell you that this may be used in evidence.' Robinson, still believing he'd done nothing wrong, signed the statement.

The intrigue, mystery and rumour surrounding the missing gemstones accelerated with the discovery of further diamonds.

Another fifteen were later handed to Police Inspector Peter Cameron by George Turner, a public works foreman in Broome. Turner had been given the diamonds, wrapped in a small pale green rag tied with red worsted, by Joe Albert, one of the Aborigines who had assisted in the rescue of survivors from Carnot Bay. Another two large diamonds, recovered a year after the crash at Carnot Bay, were traced back to Joe Albert.

On 18 March, a Chinese tailor from Broome, Ching Loong Dep, flew south to Perth. When he landed in Perth detectives were there to meet him, charging him with 'possessing diamonds, reasonably suspected of being stolen or otherwise illegally obtained'. Four hundred and sixty diamonds were found among his belongings. He claimed Aborigines had traded the diamonds for a shirt and a pair of trousers. Found guilty of the charge, he was fined £20 and the diamonds were confiscated.

Detective Blight decided to make his move. In all, 6136 diamonds had been recovered, and even though the exact quantity of diamonds had not been documented due to the haste in which they were packed, it was certain that many more were still missing. The Dutch were eager to recover them.

It had been a year since Palmer had scoured the wreckage of the *Pelikaan* and come up with his find. At 10 a.m. on 20 March 1943 he was arrested for the theft of the diamonds. That same day, James Mulgrue was also arrested.

Robinson had found some work helping out with maintenance at Fossil Downs Cattle Station, 180 kilometres east of Broome. He had hoped it was far enough away to exclude him from all the trouble brewing over the diamonds. He was wrong. A week after Jack Palmer's arrest, two police constables arrived at Fossil Downs and arrested Robinson. On the way to Broome, the crippled man sat silently in the back of the police car, cursing the day Jack Palmer had sailed into his life.

Chapter Twelve

THE TRIAL

By May 1943, news of the diamonds had hit the headlines. Journalists put the total value of the diamonds that left Java on Smirnoff's Dakota at a quarter of a million pounds—though it is certain this figure was exaggerated. But the diamonds Palmer handed in amounted to only about twenty-four lots, less than half of the sixty-five lots that left Java; the additional diamonds found later brought the total returned to the Dutch East Indies authorities to around thirty lots. This fuelled wild speculation in the media.

Prior to the trial of Jack Palmer, Detective Blight wrote to Jan van Holst Pellekaan, the Australian representative of the Netherlands Purchasing Commission, asking for the diamonds to be returned to Perth from the Commonwealth Bank in Melbourne for use as exhibits in the courtroom. Pellekaan informed Blight in confidence that some of the diamonds had already been sold by the Netherlands Purchasing Commission which was, at the time, attempting to raise finances to secure arms and air transport in the United States in the hope of reclaiming the East Indies. The Perth jeweller who had valued the diamonds at the outset heard from Blight that they were on the market and wrote asking if he could purchase some. Pellekaan was outraged and berated Blight for the breach of confidence.

Jack Palmer, who had spent his life escaping the confines of city life for the vast open spaces of the north, now found himself locked in a tiny stone-walled cell in one of the most oppressive prisons in Australia. Fremantle Prison was built in the 1850s to house convicts, but had been taken over by the military for the duration of the war. Jack's cell was only 1.2 metres by 2.1 metres with a crude bunk and table and a metal bucket for a toilet. The small barred window let in little light and the room was cold and dark. There was absolutely no fresh air. The memories of vivid warm colours, of red cliffs, white sandy beaches, bright sunlight and turquoise seas faded in the misery of the stone walls and iron door. He was awaiting trial for the theft of the Dakota diamonds.

James Mulgrue and Frank Robinson, because they were civilians, were taken to Barton's Mill after being transferred from Broome, a prison set up in 1942 in the bush east of Perth, with huts instead of cells, an orchard and workshop. On a cold

Wednesday morning, 12 May 1943, they were driven to the Supreme Court in Perth, with its grand columned facade. They were led into the holding cells in the bowels of the court.

The bailiff unlocked the cell door and beckoned for Palmer to follow. He could have handcuffed him but he chose not to. Jack Palmer joined his co-accused in the dock but neither Mulgrue nor Robinson acknowledged him. The cooler weather of the south played havoc with Robinson's arthritis and he could not stand without the aid of walking sticks.

Journalists scribbled shorthand on notepads as the seven male jurors were sworn in. Mulgrue's estranged wife, Lilian, joined the curious onlookers who piled into the public gallery.

Chief Justice John Northmore was notorious for his sour disposition and his florid, stern face. He was known to make even the most experienced lawyer quiver and his abrupt exchanges with counsel were legendary in legal circles. He frowned down at the accused from the bench as the Clerk of Courts read out the charges. Jack Palmer stood to attention. His lawyer, Nathanial Lappin, had advised him to wear his army uniform. So many people had lost relatives in the war that the sight of the uniform was sure to invoke sympathy.

Leonard Seaton appeared on behalf of Mulgrue and Robinson. From the beginning he requested the pair be tried separately from Palmer, but the Chief Justice refused.

Jan van Holst Pellekaan, Trade Commissioner for the Netherlands East Indies, was the first witness called to the stand. Pellekaan explained how the fear of Nazi invasion caused the diamonds to be moved from Amsterdam through Bandung to Australia. He identified the seals of the Javasche Bank and N.V. de Concurrent that had been impressed on the package in Java and later found at the site of Smirnoff's crashed plane.

Van Holst Pellekaan was also Australian representative for the Netherlands Purchasing Commission (NPC). When police had asked to use the diamonds as an exhibit at the trial, the NPC had informed them that the diamonds had been put on the market in accordance with the owners' wishes (the owners later disputed this). Pellekaan, however, had withheld some of the diamonds and presented them as exhibits.

Jeweller Charles Williams, of Dunklings in Perth, testified that he had valued the 6136 diamonds at £20,000.

Next, Major Clifford Gibson told of the arrival of beach-comber Jack Palmer at his office in Broome, and his surprise delivery of a substantial portion of the diamonds. When cross-examined by Lappin, Gibson described Palmer as 'uneducated rather than simple'.

Then Captain Ivan Smirnoff took the stand. More than a year had passed since he had fled Java and crash-landed in Australia's north. His injuries still plagued him, and while he had continued to fly for a few weeks after his return to Sydney, KNILM, the East Indies arm of KLM, had been coerced into selling their aircraft to the US Air Force in May 1942. Without planes to fly, Smirnoff was grounded for almost a year along with other Dutch pilots. At every opportunity, he had begged for the chance to fly for the Americans until eventually they had given in and allowed him to fly transport planes to active bases in the Pacific. He was given leave to attend the trial.

The courtroom was silent as Smirnoff recounted the ordeal of his escape from Java with 'the package of great value', the deaths of three of his passengers and one of his crew, the desperation and fear on the lonely beach at Carnot Bay, their rescue and his meeting in Melbourne with the director of the Commonwealth Bank. Lappin thanked Smirnoff for his story, and pointed out he had used the word 'hallucination' on more than one occasion. Smirnoff felt the lawyer was throwing doubt over his story. He was offended by the insinuation that he might have imagined parts of what happened. Nonetheless the events surrounding the disappearance of the package of diamonds were not clear in his mind—so much had happened on the beach that parts of it were just a blur. He reluctantly agreed with the lawyer that he had used the word 'hallucination' on a number of occasions.

Questions were raised about the integrity of the men on board the Dakota, but both Detective Blight and Ernst Smits from the Javasche Bank testified that the survivors from Carnot Bay had been put through the mill and come up clean.

Jack Palmer's case was not helped by heated exchanges between his lawyer, Nathanial Lappin, and Chief Justice Northmore. When Lappin questioned the Aboriginal couple who had crewed on Palmer's lugger the day he discovered the diamonds, Bonnie Bundigora and Tinker, the Chief Justice ordered Lappin to 'drop the pidgin English and trickery'. Bonnie remembered the trip and that Palmer had carried a parcel out from the plane, but she had not seen the diamonds.

James Mulgrue then took the stand. He told his version of the escape from Broome in the days following the Japanese air raid, and of the meeting with Palmer. Mulgrue said he had no idea if Palmer had had any intention of retaining any of the diamonds for his own use. Next, Frank Robinson said he had believed that, as the diamonds were salvage, they were at Palmer's disposal to give away or otherwise do as he liked. Robinson said he had intended to hand his share in until Palmer told him to say nothing. He thought that if he gave them to the soldiers 'it might confuse things'.

Crown Prosecutor Gordan D'Arcy raised his eyebrow. 'Might implicate someone else?'

'No,' Robinson replied unconvincingly.

'Might implicate you?' D'Arcy continued.

'No, not exactly.'

Robinson was then asked why he didn't report the diamonds to the patrolmen who visited him at Little Bay, Cape Leveque. He answered, 'I didn't place much importance on them. I had other things to think about.'

Jack Palmer never took the witness stand. In summing up, his lawyer described Palmer as a poor simple fool who, after removing the diamonds from the plane, had no idea of their value and did not know what to do with them. A polished performer, Lappin knew how to play the jury. Lappin claimed that Palmer's statement to Detective Sergeant Blight was the truth, but Jack Palmer was 'by nature a windbag'.

Various other things which he was supposed to have said to other people amounted to nothing more than mere expulsions of wind. His attempts on several occasions to hand over the stones to the proper authorities were acts which spoke far louder than his random words. He admitted that he took possession of the diamonds and gave some away, but there is no evidence of any criminal intention on his part and he made not a penny profit out of the whole deal.

Lappin appealed to the jury to look at the soldier who stood before them. 'Though simple, he has proved himself a good and loyal soldier; he was the type the Australian Army wanted.' Facing the jury, Lappin continued, 'Every member of the jury should ask himself what he would do if he found himself in circumstances similar to those in which Palmer had been placed.'

Palmer stood staring up at the crest of the Supreme Court above the judge, trying to look sincere.

The prosecutor D'Arcy had empathy with the survivors of the wrecked Dakota, having survived his own gruelling ordeal in 1930 when he was a passenger on a recreational boat which sank off the coast of Rottnest Island. He was the sole survivor. He had swum for more than eight hours to reach safety. The thought that a man might profit from the tragedy of others was no doubt abhorrent to him. He told the court the three accused had enriched themselves with stones tainted with blood, and that they had created a red herring in telling the authorities that they were cooperating by handing in only a portion of the diamonds and claiming that portion to be the total amount they had found. 'Lives of people have been lost in the transport of these diamonds. The men *should* be found guilty.'

After four days of evidence, Chief Justice John Northmore calmly outlined the cases that had been put forward by both the prosecution and the defence. He explained there was no doubt about the origin of the stones and that the actions of the accused were suspicious. He expressed regret that the majority of the stones had not been traced.

The jury retired and the journalists jumped from their seats, racing to be first to the telephones outside, as witnesses and onlookers stood in the hallway, smoking cigarettes and chatting about the evidence they had heard. 'I know what I would have done if I'd found the diamonds,' more than one person was heard to say.

Despite the judge urging the jury to take their time and consider all the evidence, they took just thirty minutes to make up their minds. The hall again filled and the crowd looked on silently in anticipation. The three accused sat waiting. So quiet was the scene that one could hear the rustle of the judge's robes as he took his seat on the bench.

Turning to the jury, the Clerk of Arraigns pronounced the familiar words, 'Do you find the accused guilty or not guilty?'

The foreman rose from his chair and drew in a deep breath before announcing the verdict: 'Not guilty.'

The Clerk of Arraigns turned to the three men in the dock. 'You are free to go, gentlemen.'

A smile spread across Palmer's face as he turned to his lawyer and then to his co-accused and shook their hands.

In his autobiography, Ivan Smirnoff recalled the judge summing up:

> You have been lucky with this finding. Whether your conscience will come to the same conclusion I cannot judge but I can tell you this, that under circumstances such as these which have been explained to us, the sudden discovery of these immeasurable riches in the wreckage on a lonely beach would have been too great a temptation for any man.

Smirnoff thought he saw the wisp of a smile around the judge's mouth and surmised that the old man possessed a large measure of knowledge about human nature.

As the doors swung wide for them, the three men waved cheerfully to sympathisers in the public gallery. 'Diamond' Jack Palmer, as he became known, smiled—he was a free man and from that day forward was never without a quid.

The trial was one of the most celebrated of the era and generated publicity nationwide, the newspapers labelling the story 'as bizarre and sensational as any best-selling thriller'. From Albany to Wyndham and across the country to Sydney, Melbourne and Brisbane, people speculated about the fate of the missing diamonds. Most people believed Diamond Jack had hidden away some of the treasure.

Outside the court, Captain Smirnoff leant against the wall deep in thought, drawing back on a cigarette. He felt someone touch his arm and turned to see Ernst Smits from the Javasche Bank. He asked the captain if he was surprised, to which Smirnoff replied, 'I have known a moment in my life when a human being would be justified in asking himself what the real value of diamonds is, and in the past year I have seen many things that make me wonder about this still.'

The trial was the culmination of a miserable year for Smirnoff. Aside from the trauma of Carnot Bay, his wife's cancer had worsened, and the former war hero and world-renowned aviator had suffered the humiliation of almost a year's unemployment. While the war in the Pacific had begun to turn around in favour of the Allies, there was no immediate end in sight. When compared to things like peace, health and security, the value of the diamonds no doubt seemed insignificant to Smirnoff— though he wondered what happened to the remainder until the day he died.

Chapter Thirteen

DIAMOND FEVER

In the end, the diamonds returned to the Dutch East Indies Trade Commissioner, Jan van Holst Pellekaan, had an estimated value today of more than A$20 million. An even greater amount has never been recovered. As Carnot Bay survivor Leon Vanderburg said before his death in 1975, 'Personally, I do not doubt that quite some fortune in diamonds has still been unaccounted for, possibly buried in the sand at the place where several lives were lost.'

At the height of diamond talk in the Kimberley, the belief that these gems might lie buried somewhere along the coastline between Broome and Cape Leveque led to frenzied searches. When a showboat full of magician's trinkets—including rings with imitation diamonds, and cigar boxes full of different coloured glass beads—sailed close to Beagle Bay, the local Aborigines, believing they were valuable gemstones, rushed to the coast in droves and stripped the boat bare, leaving it stranded. Glass beads and imitation diamonds soon circulated throughout the Kimberley. Some were handed in to police.

In the book *Port of Pearls*, author Hugh Edwards wrote that a young married Aboriginal couple, who had been given a house at Beagle Bay, asked permission to demolish it because they believed a tin of diamonds was plastered into one of the walls. In another story, a handyman offered to carry out renovations to the home of Broome resident Jack Pryor at a ridiculously low price, but when Pryor went to check on the progress of the work, the handyman had gone. The job was left unfinished and there was a small hole in the fireplace where he had been working. It was said that diamonds were hidden in the niche and that the handyman, whoever he was, had finally built up the courage to collect what he had kept hidden for years. Other diamonds were said to have been found in the fork of a tree.

Several expeditions have dug through the wells at Beagle Bay, but no diamonds have been discovered. In general, the remoteness and vastness of the area daunted many of those seeking an easy prize, the distance and terrain forcing them to retreat defeated.

Diamonds were part of the Kimberley folklore well before Jack Palmer's find—several stories whispered of a fortune buried beneath the land. For example, before the outbreak of the Second World War, the Benedictine monks at Kalumburu

Mission on the northern tip of the Kimberley were handed a quantity of stones purported to be rough diamonds by a man named Watson. He wouldn't identify where they had come from. But on his deathbed Watson handed raw diamonds to a Sydney jeweller and told him the location—he described a mountain with one side crumbled away where a fortune in diamonds could be found. A search by professional geologists, along with the Benedictine monks and the Aborigines from the area, failed to find the fabled jewels.

Ironically, as treasure hunters scoured the region—first for Watson's and later Palmer's diamonds—lying beneath the ancient rocks and creekbeds of the Kimberley lay a fortune in diamonds. A rich alluvial pipe discovered to the south-east of Kalumburu in 1979 would lead to the development of the world's largest single producer of diamonds, the Argyle Diamond Mine. Their diamonds are renowned for their unique brilliance and stunning array of colours, from the rare pink to the classic white and sparkling champagne. Today, the mine produces approximately one third of the world's supply of natural diamonds, although only 5 per cent are gem quality. And near Derby, a town that Jack Palmer visited regularly while sailing the coast in his lugger the *Eurus*, another mine at Ellendale is predicted to become the fifth-largest diamond producer in the world.

Soon after the trial of Diamond Jack Palmer, Ivan Smirnoff travelled to the United States, where KLM was running a service of big Lockheed L.14s from Miami. The press were there to meet him and he was soon booked for a series of lectures across the country.

Late in 1943, Hollywood film director Cecil B. De Mille approached Smirnoff, hoping to put the story of his life up on the big screen. Smirnoff was at first delighted until he met the actor De Mille chose to play him. 'I am a pilot, I am an experienced man, everybody knows it. People see me in a film as a damn silly youngster, they don't fly with me any more.' He refused to budge and the project was called off.

A month later a representative of Sir Alexander Korda, who at that time was the executive producer of the English division of MGM, approached Smirnoff, anxious to buy the film rights of the book being written about his life with the help of a Netherlands government official. By that time, Smirnoff was so concerned the motion picture treatment would make him look like 'a gigolo' that he would not entertain the idea. Smirnoff had also been arguing with the government official and the manuscript had been scrapped.

His wounds played up and he ended up back in hospital where the bullets he received over the Australian coast were finally removed. Smirnoff and his wife Margot returned to the Netherlands in September 1945. Margot was overjoyed to return to Amsterdam, where she and Ivan had spent so many happy days. Margot's battle with cancer ended on 3 July 1946. In her final days, her husband never left her side. After a long bout of depression, he completed the story of his life, titled *De*

Toekomst heeft Vleugels (The Future has Wings). He eventually remarried and moved to Spain. In 1956 he died of cancer in Palma, Majorca. His body was later exhumed and reburied in the Netherlands next to Margot's.

After the trial, Jim Mulgrue returned to Broome, working in various local stores. On the morning of 14 February 1957 a cyclone passed directly over the town. Jim, then aged eighty-one, was sitting in his house when he heard the roaring rage of the gale-force winds as they uprooted trees, ripped up metal and tossed debris into the air. Frustratingly, he couldn't see what was going on. He had become blind and disorientated in his old age and the sound was deafening and disturbing. Then it was quiet for a short while as the eye of the cyclone passed over. A minute later part of the walls and roof of his home collapsed and Jim was trapped unconscious beneath the rubble. He was rescued and taken to Broome hospital, but he never regained consciousness. He died alone without a penny to his name.

Frank Robinson had not allowed his crippling arthritis to chain him down. He had travelled the world, from port to port, never staying in one place for long, and the prospect of long-term incarceration would have weighed heavily on his mind. He must have decided at some time during the trial to move far away from Broome. The author has been unable to trace his final resting place.

Beset by health problems, Jack Palmer was discharged from the military forces in December 1943, seven months after the trial. Many locals thought Diamond Jack was 'the richest man in Broome'. After the war he bought a blue Chevrolet he called Bluebird, and a house in Wallcott Street, which he purchased outright and later swapped for another house a few streets away. He worked now and then but mostly continued what he liked doing best: fishing, beachcombing and hunting for dugong.

On one occasion he gave about a dozen wharf labourers their entire wages from a roll of notes he pulled from his pocket when their pay was late arriving at the jetty office. He was also said to spend quite a bit of money satisfying his sexual urges. When asked by a friend what he had done with the diamonds, he grinned. 'It helps keep the gins happy.'

Plagued by cancer in his later years, Palmer was cared for by the Sisters of St John of God in Perth and in Broome. On his deathbed in 1958, 62-year-old Palmer was asked by a priest what he had really done with the rest of the diamonds. Smiling broadly, Palmer replied that he had handed them all over to the authorities. He was said to have had well over £1000 in the bag at his bedside, but the money disappeared the day after he died. His house was left to the local baker, Phillip Cox.

Now buried beneath the sand at Carnot Bay, a plaque commemorates the crash of Smirnoff's Dakota. A few remnants of the ill-fated plane can still be seen at low tide, and a metal cross on the beach marks the place where Maria van Tuyn, Jo van Tuyn, Daan Hendriksz and Joop Blaauw lost their lives.

The place is remote and almost impossible to get to, with only a handful of local residents able and willing to locate the desolate shore. Travel must be by day to find the rugged tracks through dense bush and soft sand. Not even the hardiest of four-wheel-drive vehicles can make it all the way to the remote beach. When the rough track runs out, there is still a five-kilometre walk in the blazing sun to reach the crash site, and that walk can take place only if you arrive on low tide.

Despite the difficulty of the terrain, a few have travelled to the beach. Over the years pieces from the plane were removed as souvenirs, while other parts washed away on the tide. In the mid-1970s a group of young men came across the wreck. They filled the plane with explosives and blew it up for the fun of it.

Treasure hunters still visit the remote north-west coast in the hope of one day finding the missing diamonds. But if Palmer's diamonds have brought anyone else fortune, they have learnt from Palmer's mistake and not whispered a word about their find.

At Beagle Bay, the Aborigines still tell of the time when, as children, they played marbles with the diamonds, and their parents traded treasure for tobacco. Many believe that there are still diamonds to be found at the bottom of the wells or springs around Beagle Bay.

At Broome's town beach, a tiny graveyard with rusty fence rails and faded headstones sits atop a grassy hill under shady trees overlooking Roebuck Bay. Set apart from the grander headstones is a small modern plaque marked 'Diamond Jack', the only memorial to the larrikin who sailed the northern shores and found a great treasure.

EPILOGUE

On the night of 21 August 1945, Japanese soldiers lined the streets of Bandung in Java to protect the long column of sick, wounded and dying internees carried on stretchers by men themselves so enfeebled that they could hardly stay upright. Among the weary bodies that marched towards the railway station and home were the owners of the diamonds, Willy Olberg and David Davidson. It seemed at that moment that peace would be restored to their world—but the world had changed dramatically and nothing would be as it was before, for Indonesia was about to go through its most turbulent years of the century as the Dutch battled to re-establish authority against the rising tide of nationalist sentiment.

The Second World War came to an end on 15 August 1945—the Japanese announced their unconditional surrender after the United States of America dropped atom bombs on

Hiroshima and Nagasaki—but in Indonesia a new battle had begun. Before the Japanese surrendered they had promised to grant Indonesia independence, and on 17 August Sukarno and Mohammed Hatta announced the Declaration for the Republic of Indonesia.

Dutch government officials had hoped to restore the country to its old ways and called on the British and Japanese to assist. An estimated 70,000 Dutch men, women and children had been interned when the Japanese took over Indonesia, but as word spread of the Japanese surrender the internees began to break out of the internment camps. Insurgent nationalist groups rounded up some of the escaped internees and in many cases murdered them. Bewildered and rebellious, the nationalists' sense of resentment against the Dutch was heightened by Japanese propaganda and by what the Japanese had extracted from them during the war years. The Red Cross reported that the majority of Dutch people in Indonesia were 'in imminent danger of being massacred'.

Willy Olberg was reunited with his daughter, Elly, but his son, Frans, did not come home. Willy and Elly embarked on a desperate search, and were advised Frans had been found in a POW camp in Sumatra but had been urgently evacuated to hospital in Singapore. It was thought he would not survive the journey. Frans was suffering from starvation, dehydration, malaria and tropical ulcers, which had eaten through flesh, muscle, tendon and bone; he was blind in both eyes. He had been among the thousands of British and Dutch servicemen who had laboured for eighteen hours a day on a narrow gauge railway in the central portion of Sumatra. More than 700 of these servicemen died.

Frans's family flew to Singapore expecting to say their farewells, but in the following months he slowly made a remarkable recovery. However his keen eyesight, the most important tool of his trade as a diamond valuer, was gone forever. Instead, images from the camp would remain vividly etched on his mind: starvation, torture, disease, beatings and beheadings. 'To keep my sanity I look forward, not backward,' Frans Olberg told the author in 2005, 'but I can't control my head at night.'

David Davidson was reunited with his wife and four children, including his youngest son, John Frans Bernard Eduard, born the day the Japanese took over Bandung.

Willy Olberg and David Davidson were eager to rebuild their lives and those of their families, and to try to put the horrors of war behind them. Control of their business was given back to them. They had hidden a few jewels and concealed gold inside enamel plates when the Japanese marched on Bandung. They retrieved the jewels, and the enamel shells of the plates from which the Japanese had eaten were smashed, revealing their solid gold cores. The firm again began to fashion the fine pieces of jewellery for which it was famous.

In 1946 Willy Olberg travelled to Australia, hoping to retrieve the diamonds from the Commonwealth Bank in Melbourne. But he was taken aback by the news that the diamonds had been sold and only a pittance in cash remained to compensate him. He was sceptical about the story regarding the loss of the diamonds, and sceptical too about the sale price. The agreement signed by the directors of N.V. de Concurrent had made the diamonds available to the Netherlands East Indies government and empowered it to dispose of them. But it was never Olberg's nor Davidson's intention that the diamonds be sold. Returning to Bandung, Olberg began legal action against the Netherlands East Indies authorities.

The locals in Indonesia were resentful at the return of the Dutch to their businesses and N.V. de Concurrent was frequently targeted by angry youths. Facing the return of Dutch colonial rule, in what became known as 'Bandung Lautan Api' (Bandung Ocean of Fire) the Indonesian citizens of Bandung chose to burn the city down rather than hand it back. They fled to the hills, watching as an ocean of flames swept over their home. There they penned 'Halo, Halo, Bandung', the anthem promising their return. Most of the southern part of the city was destroyed. N.V. de Concurrent survived but attacks on the business continued. As the Dutch became more ruthless in attempting to repress the independence movement, reprisals became fiercer. When the safe was blown up and the shop completely looted of every item of jewellery and cash, the families who had built up the store knew it was time to leave.

Five years of violence and fighting culminated in the creation of the Republic of Indonesia in 1950, with an estimated 300,000 Dutch citizens leaving the island in its wake. The Olberg and Davidson families eventually sold up during the 1950s and emigrated to Canada, Australia and Amsterdam. There was no longer a Netherlands East Indies government to sue.

Over the years the Olbergs and Davidsons talked of expeditions to Broome to try to recover the diamonds, but these never eventuated. Relatives contacted the Dutch consul in Western Australia asking that if any diamonds were recovered they be returned to the family, but no further diamonds were handed in.

In the 1980s, two men offered to recover the diamonds for Olberg's daughter, Elly, who resides in Sydney, Australia. The treasure hunters weren't prepared to take a commission, wanting money up front. She refused.

BIBLIOGRAPHY

Books

Bailey, J. (2001) *The White Divers of Broome*. Sydney, PanMacmillan.

Bain, M. A. (1982) *Full Fathom Five*. Perth, Artlook Books.

Banfield, E. J. (1908) *Confessions of a Beachcomber*. Sydney, Angus & Robertson.

Bartlett, N. (1954) *The Pearl Seekers*. London, Andrew Melrose Ltd.

Byrne, G. & Bolton, G. (2005) *May it Please Your Honour: A history of the Supreme Court of Western Australia, 1861–2005*. Perth, Scott Print.

Choo, C. (2001) *Mission Girls: Aboriginal Women on Catholic Missions in the Kimberley, Western Australia 1900–1950*. Perth, University of Western Australia Press.

Coupar, A. (1960) *The Smirnoff Story*. London, Jarrolds.

Duyken, E. (1987) *The Dutch in Australia*. Melbourne, AE Press.

Edwards, H. (1984) *Port of Pearls: Broome's First One Hundred Years*, Perth, Hugh Edwards.

Edwards, H. (1991) *Kimberley: Dreaming to Diamonds*. Perth, Hugh Edwards.

Epstein, E. (1982) *The Rise and Fall of Diamonds*. New York, Simon & Schuster.

Faine, J. (1992) *Taken on Oath—A Generation of Lawyers*. Sydney, Federation Press.

Idriess, Ion L. (1937) *Forty Fathoms Deep*. Sydney, Angus & Robertson.

Prime, M. (1992) *Broome's One Day War: The Story of the Japanese Raid on Broome 3rd March 1942*. Broome, Broome Historical Society.

Smirnoff, I. (1947) *De Toekomst heeft Vleugels* [*The Future has Wings*].
  Amsterdam, Elsevier.
Tyler, W. H. (1986) *Flight of Diamonds*. Perth, Hesperian Press.
van der Post, L. (1996) *The Admiral's Baby*. London, John Murray.

Articles

The West Australian, April–May 1943.
The Northern Times, May 1943.
Daily News, undated article, interview with Major Clifford Gibson (held by the
  Broome Historical Society).
Bussemaker, H. (1996) 'Australian Dutch Defence Cooperation 1940–41'. *Journal
  of the Australian War Memorial* (29).
Dijkstra, N. (1994) 'Under the Sydney Harbour Bridge'. 18th Squadron Newsletter,
  July.
Henderson, J. (1979) 'Diamonds are (Missing) Forever'. *Australian Playboy*,
  November.
Toohey, P. (2005) 'When War Came to Australia: Our Secret History'. *The
  Bulletin*, 13 April.

Archive material

Trial transcripts, Supreme Court of Western Australia, trial of Jack Palmer, James
  Mulgrue and Frank Robinson, May 1943.
De Javasche Bank diamonds, Secretary's Department General Correspondence,
  Commonwealth Bank Records, 1942–1943.
Letter to Commissioner of Police [*JDC typed at base of letter*], 5 March 1945,
  State Archives of Western Australia.
Police Service Records of James Duff Cowie, Peter Meikle Cameron and
  Detective A. R. Blight, Western Australian Police Historical Society.
Lilian Mulgrue interview, Oral History Transcript, Battye Library Western
  Australian Collection, 27 August 1981.
'The Story of What Happened to 205 Squadron at Broome, Western Australia'
  (with some extracts from Appendix 1 to the 205 Squadron Log), undated
  and author not noted, Broome Historical Society.

Written accounts from survivors of the Broome air raid

Henri Marinus Juta, Instituut voor Maritieme Historie, The Hague.
Sophia van Tour, Instituut voor Maritieme Historie, The Hague.
Lucas Bruinsma, D. Swierstra, The Netherlands, 1990.
Lt Cornelis Fekke Amsterdam, D. Swierstra, The Netherlands, 1990.
Frederika Wilhehnina van Emmerik, D. Swierstra, The Netherlands, 1990.
Frits Julius Wissel, D. Swierstra, The Netherlands, 1990.
Marjorie Bardwell, Broome Historical Society, Western Australia, 1971.
Catharina Komen-Blommert & Hans Komen, Broome Historical Society,
     Western Australia, 2000.
Robert Lacomble, 1992 (author).
Constable Leslie William Menhennett, undated account of Japanese raids on
     Broome, Broome Historical Society, Western Australia.
Elly Koens, Broome Historical Society, Western Australia, 2002.
Mrs Doorman, Broome Historical Society, Western Australia.

Other written accounts

Brother Richard Bessenfelder, La Grange, Battye Library, 1977.
Leon Vanderburg, 1972 (W. H. Tyler, *Flight of Diamonds*, 1986).

Web pages

'Australia's War 1939–1945 Fall of Java', Australian Government Department of
     Veteran Affairs Commonwealth of Australia, 2000.
     www.ww2australia.gov.au/japadvance/qantas.html
Biemond, A. (2004) 'A guest of the Japanese in the Dutch Indies', moderated
     WWII newsgroup posted by Dan Ford. *www.warbirdforum.com/biemond.htm*
Birrell, F. (2002) 'The History of the Beagle Bay Mission'.
     www.shsbeaglebay.wa.edu.au/history.htm
Duffy, G. (2000) 'Life and Death on the Death Railway through the Jungles of
     Sumatra'. *www.usmm.org/duffylifedeath.html*
Dunn, P. (2000) 'Crash of a Japanese Fighter Aircraft; Destruction of Fifteen
     Flying Boats, Two B-17 Flying Fortresses, Two B-24 Liberators, Two

Lockheed Hudsons, Two Dc-3's and a Lockheed Lodestar on 3 March 1942 During A Japanese Air Raid On Broome'. *home.st.net.au/~dunn/wa12.htm*

Dunn, P. (2000) 'Captain Ivan Smirnoff'. *home.st.net.au/~dunn/smirnoff.htm*

Ganse, A. (2001; rev. 2004) 'World War II: Dutch East India'. World History at KMLA. *www.zum.de/whkmla/region/seasia/wwiidei.html*

Gibbs, J. A. & Jenkins (Captain) S. (1998) 'Western Australia The War Years 1939–1945'. *www2.tpg.com.au/users/vk6pg/vk6sig/waryears.htm#1942*

Graham, W. B. (2001) 'Empire C Class Flying Boats'. *www.adf-serials.com*

Jubbs, L. (2001) 'The Forgotten Era of Men and Vessels'. *www.futurepd.org/les/Documents/NewBook%20F.pdf*

Klemen, L. (2001) 'The Forgotten Campaign: The Dutch East Indies Campaign 1941–1942'. *www.geocities.com/dutcheastindies/*

Klemen, L. (1999–2002) 'The conquest of Java Island March 1942'. *www.geocities.com/dutcheastindies/java.html*

Kroupnik, V. 'The Incredible Adventure of the Russian Airman Ivan Smirnoff in Australia'. *www.argo.net.au/andre/smirnovENFIN.htm*

Lewendon, R. J. 'Extracts from Gunners in Java—1942'. COFEPOW—The Children (& Families) of the Far East Prisoners of War. *www.cofepow.org.uk/pages/asia_java2.htm*

Lockwood, R. (1970) 'Indonesian Exiles in Australia 1942–47'. *66.102.7.104/search?q=cache:8qoYNZRJszsJ:e-publishing.library.cornell.edu/DPubS/Repository/1.0/Disseminate/seap.indo/1107123627/body/pdf*

McCarthy, M., Green, J., Jung, S. and Souter, C. (2002) 'The Broome flying boats: Papers relating to the nomination of a suite of World War II flying boat wrecks in Broome to the Register of Heritage Places under the *Heritage of Western Australia Act 1990*', report, Department of Maritime Archeology, WA Maritime Museum. *66.102.7.104/search?q=cache:ZXP0uyzALuUJ:www.museum.wa.gov.au/mm/Museum/march/fallenangels/broome.doc*

Mackersey, I. (1999) 'Smithy'. *www.ianmackersey.com/kingsford_smith_book/kingsford_smith_book.html*

Michman, D. (2004) '"Turquoise, Sapphire and Diamond" to "Mazal U'brachah": Jews in the Diamond Trade in Modern History'. Bar-Ilan University Torah portion. *www.biu.ac.il/JH/Parasha/eng/tetzaveh/michman.html*

Modern History Sourcebook. 'Pearl Harbor Attack Documents, 1941 From: Navy Department To: CinCUS, Pearl Harbor Date: 27 Nov. 41'. *www.fordham.edu/halsall/mod/1941PEARL.html*

Oliver, P. (2004) 'Interpreting "Japanese Activities" in Australia 1888–1945'. *Australian War Memorial Journal, www.awm.gov.au/journal/j36/oliver.htm*

Taylan, J. and Kessling, D. 'Kalidjati (Kalijati, Karichagi) Airfield'. Pacific Wrecks 1997–2005. *www.pacificwrecks.com*

US Army Center of Military History (2003) 'The East Indies'. CMH Pub 72–22. *www.army.mil/cmh-pg/brochures/eindies/eindies.htm*

Wallace, R. R. (2001) 'The Gold Vault in Broken Hill Gaol'. Broken Hill Historical Society.
www.peoplesvoice.gov.au/stories/nsw/brokenhill/brokenhill_w_gold.htm

Western Australian Museum (2003) 'Zero Hour, 3rd March 1942'.
www.museum.gov.au/mm/Museum/march/treasures/zerohour/doco_a.html

Interviews

Pieter Cramerus, interviewed by Juliet Wills, 2005.

Carel Davidson (son of David Davidson), interviewed by Juliet Wills, 2005.

Flora Davidson (daughter of David Davidson), interviewed by Juliet Wills, 2005.

Jo Muller, interviewed by Thom Olink, *Haagse Courant*, 1972.

Gus Winckel, interviewed by Juliet Wills, 2005, and Marianne van Velzen, 2004.

Henk Hasselo, interviewed by Marianne van Velzen, 2004, and Juliet Wills, 2005.

Elly Doeland (nee Koens), interviewed by Juliet Wills, 2005.

Father Kevin McKelson, interviewed by Juliet Wills, 2005.

Elly Festinger (nee Olberg), interviewed by Juliet Wills, 2005.

Frans Olberg, interviewed by Juliet Wills, 2005.

Willy Piers (grandson of Cornelia Piers, who died in Broome on 3 March 1942), interviewed by Juliet Wills and Marianne van Velzen, 2005.

Daryll and Cheryl Mulgrue (grandchildren of James and Lilian Mulgrue), interviewed by Juliet Wills, 2005.

ACKNOWLEDGMENTS

Thank you to the following people and institutions for their assistance in producing this book:

Pieter Cramerus—his assistance in writing this book has been priceless.

Historian Mervyn Prime, whose dedication in recording the events and collecting photographs and personal accounts of the Broome air raid have ensured that this part of Australia's history is not forgotten.

Stephen Fleay, Bandung, Indonesia, for photographs and descriptions of locations in Bandung.

The Broome Historical Society for answering an endless round of questions and providing photographs and published material.

The Battye Library, Western Australia.

Thomas Dercksen, former Dutch Consul in Western Australia for assisting in translation of *De Toekomst heeft Vleugels*.

Arrow Pearl Farms and Pearl Luggers Museum, Broome, for accommodation in Beagle Bay and assistance with research.

Dave McKenzie, Arrow Pearl Farms, Beagle Bay, for assisting in the search for the crash site at Carnot Bay.

L. Klemen and B. Kossen, webmaster: 'Forgotten Campaign: The Dutch East Indies Campaign 1941–1942', for locating historical information.

Father Bernard Arnali, Beagle Bay.

The Beagle Bay community.

The Daan family, Broome.

Sue Poelina, Broome.

Veteran Wireless Operators Association.

The Western Australia Police.

Tracy Howard, Middle Lagoon, Western Australia for her expert knowledge of the area.

John Wills and Graeme Charlwood.